CHERISHED

21
DESIGNS
BY
KIM
HARGREAVES

CREDITS

DESIGNS & STYLING
Kim Hargreaves

EDITOR
Kathleen Hargreaves

HAIR & MAKE-UP
Diana Fisher

MODEL
Kristie Stubley

PHOTOGRAPHY
Graham Watts

LAYOUTS
Angela Lin

PATTERNS
Sue Whiting & Trisha McKenzie

Published in 2010 by Kim Hargreaves
Intake Cottage
26 Underbank Old Road
Holmfirth
West Yorkshire
HD9 1EA
England

British Library Cataloguing in Publication Data
A catalogue record for this book is available from the British Library

ISBN   1-906487-09-6
ISBN–13   978-1-906487-09-6

CONTENTS

WITH A
CHILL
IN THE AIR,
WINTER DRAWS
EVER CLOSER....

Wrap up in layers of love worn threads
to defy the season's icy breath.
In a rural setting, deep textures and
soft femininity blend with masculine
lines to create a cosy gathering.

This page, FORD a
classic trench coat
with cable detail,
opposite, RIVER
ribbed mini skirt
with shaping detail

10

PAGE a short sleeved
chunky textured edge
to edge jacket

12

HEATH a pretty
open stitch scarf worked
in mohair & silk

14

This page, HEATH
& MYSTERY
an open stitch scarf
& classic cardigan,
opposite, SKYLARK
a lace ribbed cardigan
with soft neckline

This page FOREST
a double-breasted
coat with epaulets,
opposite, EDEN
a close-fitting
textured hat

LUNA a pretty
raglan cardigan with
beaded lace edging

EMBER a jacket
with snug collar, deep
texture & epaulet
details

26

COMET a close-fitting
capped sleeved vest &
open stitch snood

BOUNTY
a neat fitting shrug
with front ties

ISLE a fitted double-breasted cardigan with box pleats, worn with EDEN a close-fitting hat

34

WISDOM a neat cardigan worked in bands of double moss stitch along with contrasting coloured details

37

WINTER a cape style
coat featuring curved
hemline, worn with
MOON a slouchy hat

WINTER a generous
coat with pockets &
MOON a slouchy
lace panelled hat

RAINE a neat
shawl collared
double-breasted
peplum cardigan

MOON a slouchy
lace panelled hat

46

FAYER a snuggly
understated sweater
with generous neck

This page,
CLARITY a
soft & cosy crochet
scarf, opposite,
FAWN an
understated
cropped classic
cardigan

FAWN an understated cropped cardigan, worn with CLARITY a lacy scarf

GOODWILL a
tweedy jacket with
covered buttons &
crochet trims, worn
with MOON a
slouchy lace hat

55

THE
PATTERNS

Recommendation

Suitable for the knitter with a little experience
Please see pages 8, 9 & 10 for photographs.

	XS	S	M	L	XL	XXL	
To fit	**81**	**86**	**91**	**97**	**102**	**109**	cm
bust	32	34	36	38	40	43	in

Rowan Felted Tweed Aran

21 22 24 25 27 29 x 50gm
Photographed in Pebble

Needles

1 pair 4mm (no 8) (US 6) needles
1 pair 4½mm (no 7) (US 7) needles
1 pair 5mm (no 6) (US 8) needles
Cable needle

Extras – 14 large and 2 smaller buttons, one
5 cm (2 in) buckle and pair of shoulder pads
(optional)

Tension

17 sts and 25 rows to 10 cm measured over
textured pattern using 5mm (US 8) needles.

Special abbreviations

C6B = slip next 3 sts onto cn and leave at
back of work, K3, then K3 from cn; **C6F** = slip
next 3 sts onto cn and leave at front of work,
K3, then K3 from cn; **C8B** = slip next 4 sts
onto cn and leave at back of work, K4, then
K4 from cn; **C8F** = slip next 4 sts onto cn and
leave at front of work, K4, then K4 from cn;
C10B = slip next 5 sts onto cn and leave at
back of work, K5, then K5 from cn; **C10F** = slip
next 5 sts onto cn and leave at front of work,
K5, then K5 from cn; **cn** = cable needle.

FORD
CLASSIC BELTED TRENCH COAT WITH MANY DETAILS

BACK

Cast on 99 (103: 107: 111: 115: 123) sts
using 5mm (US 8) needles.
Row 1 (RS): P1, (P1, K1 tbl) 7 (8: 9: 10: 11:
13) times, *(K2, inc in next st, K1) twice, P1,
(K1, inc in next st, K2) twice*, (K1 tbl, P1)
17 times, K1 tbl, rep from * to * once more,
(K1 tbl, P1) 7 (8: 9: 10: 11: 13) times, P1.
107 (111: 115: 119: 123: 131) sts.
Row 2: K15 (17: 19: 21: 23: 27), P10, K1,
P10, K35, P10, K1, P10, K15 (17: 19: 21:
23: 27).
Row 3: P1, (P1, K1 tbl) 7 (8: 9: 10: 11: 13)
times, K10, P1, K10, (K1 tbl, P1) 17 times,
K1 tbl, K10, P1, K10, (K1 tbl, P1) 7 (8: 9: 10:
11: 13) times, P1.
Last 2 rows set the sts.
Cont as now set for a further 15 rows, ending
with a WS row.
Row 19 (RS): Patt 15 (17: 19: 21: 23: 27) sts,
C10B, P1, C10F, patt 35 sts, C10B, P1, C10F,
patt 15 (17: 19: 21: 23: 27) sts.
Work 19 rows, dec 1 st at each end of 8th
of these rows and ending with a WS row.
105 (109: 113: 117: 121: 129) sts.
Row 39: Patt 14 (16: 18: 20: 22: 26) sts,
C10B, P1, C10F, patt 35 sts, C10B, P1, C10F,
patt 14 (16: 18: 20: 22: 26) sts.
Work 17 rows, dec 1 st at each end of 2nd and
foll 14th row and ending with a WS row. 101
(105: 109: 113: 117: 125) sts.
Row 57: Patt 12 (14: 16: 18: 20: 24) sts, *slip
next 5 sts onto cn and leave at back of work,
K3, K2tog, then K2tog, K3 across 5 sts on cn,
P1, slip next 5 sts onto cn and leave at front
of work, K3, K2tog, then K2tog, K3 across 5 sts
on cn*, patt 35 sts, rep from * to * once more,
patt 12 (14: 16: 18: 20: 24) sts.
93 (97: 101: 105: 109: 117) sts.
Now working 8 sts in each cable panel instead
of 10 sts, work 15 rows, dec 1 st at each
end of 12th of these rows and ending with
a WS row.
91 (95: 99: 103: 107: 115) sts.
Row 73: Patt 11 (13: 15: 17: 19: 23) sts, C8B,
P1, C8F, patt 35 sts, C8B, P1, C8F, patt 11 (13:
15: 17: 19: 23) sts.
Work 15 rows, dec 1 st at each end of 10th
of these rows and ending with a WS row.
89 (93: 97: 101: 105: 113) sts.

Row 89: Patt 10 (12: 14: 16: 18: 22) sts, C8B,
P1, C8F, patt 35 sts, C8B, P1, C8F, patt 10 (12:
14: 16: 18: 22) sts.
Work 13 rows, dec 1 st at each end of 8th of
these rows and ending with a WS row.
87 (91: 95: 99: 103: 111) sts.
Row 103: Patt 9 (11: 13: 15: 17: 21) sts, *slip
next 4 sts onto cn and leave at back of work,
K2, K2tog, then K2tog, K2 across 4 sts on cn,
P1, slip next 4 sts onto cn and leave at front
of work, K2, K2tog, then K2tog, K2 across 4 sts
on cn*, patt 35 sts, rep from * to * once more,
patt 9 (11: 13: 15: 17: 21) sts.
79 (83: 87: 91: 95: 103) sts.
Now working 6 sts in each cable panel instead
of 8 sts, work 11 rows, ending with a WS row.
Row 115: Patt 9 (11: 13: 15: 17: 21) sts, C6B,
P1, C6F, patt 35 sts, C6B, P1, C6F, patt 9 (11:
13: 15: 17: 21) sts.
Last 12 rows form patt for rest of back.
Cont in patt, inc 1 st at each end of 22nd
and foll 16th row, taking inc sts into patt.
83 (87: 91: 95: 99: 107) sts.
Cont straight until back measures 66 (66: 67:
67: 67: 67) cm, ending with a WS row.
Shape armholes
Keeping patt correct, cast off 3 (3: 4: 4: 5: 6)
sts at beg of next 2 rows.
77 (81: 83: 87: 89: 95) sts.
Dec 1 st at each end of next 3 (3: 3: 5: 5: 7)
rows, then on foll 2 (3: 3: 2: 2: 2) alt rows,
then on foll 4th row.
65 (67: 69: 71: 73: 75) sts.
Cont straight until armhole measures 19 (20:
20: 21: 22: 23) cm, ending with a WS row.
Shape shoulders and back neck
Cast off 7 (7: 7: 7: 8: 8) sts at beg of next
2 rows.
51 (53: 55: 57: 57: 59) sts.
Next row (RS): Cast off 7 (7: 7: 7: 8: 8) sts,
patt until there are 10 (11: 12: 12: 11: 12) sts
on right needle and turn, leaving rem sts on a
holder.
Work each side of neck separately.
Cast off 4 sts at beg of next row.
Cast off rem 6 (7: 8: 8: 7: 8) sts.
With RS facing, rejoin yarn to rem sts, cast off
centre 17 (17: 17: 19: 19: 19) sts, patt to end.
Complete to match first side, reversing
shapings.

POCKET LININGS (make 2)
Cast on 18 sts using 5mm (US 8) needles.
Starting with a K row, work in st st for 18 rows, ending with a WS row.
Break yarn and leave sts on a holder.

LEFT FRONT
Cast on 68 (70: 72: 74: 76: 80) sts using 5mm (US 8) needles.
Row 1 (RS): P1, (P1, K1 tbl) 7 (8: 9: 10: 11: 13) times, (K2, inc in next st, K1) twice, P1, (K1, inc in next st, K2) twice, (K1 tbl, P1) 16 times, K4. 72 (74: 76: 78: 80: 84) sts.
Row 2: K36, P10, K1, P10, K15 (17: 19: 21: 23: 27).
Row 3: P1, (P1, K1 tbl) 7 (8: 9: 10: 11: 13) times, K10, P1, K10, (K1 tbl, P1) 16 times, K4.
Last 2 rows set the sts.
Cont as now set for a further 15 rows, ending with a WS row.
Row 19 (RS): Patt 15 (17: 19: 21: 23: 27) sts, C10B, P1, C10F, patt 36 sts.
Work 19 rows, dec 1 st at beg of 8th of these rows and ending with a WS row.
71 (73: 75: 77: 79: 83) sts.
Row 39: Patt 14 (16: 18: 20: 22: 26) sts, C10B, P1, C10F, patt 36 sts.
Work 17 rows, dec 1 st at beg of 2nd and foll 14th row and ending with a WS row.
69 (71: 73: 75: 77: 81) sts.
Row 57: Patt 12 (14: 16: 18: 20: 24) sts, slip next 5 sts onto cn and leave at back of work, K3, K2tog, then K2tog, K3 across 5 sts on cn, P1, slip next 5 sts onto cn and leave at front of work, K3, K2tog, then K2tog, K3 across 5 sts on cn, patt 36 sts.
65 (67: 69: 71: 73: 77) sts.
Now working 8 sts in each cable panel instead of 10 sts, work 7 rows, ending with a WS row.
Place pocket
Row 65 (RS): Patt 11 (13: 15: 17: 19: 23) sts, slip rem 54 sts onto a holder (for pocket front) and, in their place, K across 18 sts of first pocket lining. 29 (31: 33: 35: 37: 41) sts.
Keeping pocket lining sts in st st and side front sts in patt as set, dec 1 st at beg of 4th and 2 foll 14th rows.
26 (28: 30: 32: 34: 38) sts.
Work a further 7 rows, ending with a WS row.
Row 105 (RS): Patt 8 (10: 12: 14: 16: 20) sts, cast off rem 18 sts.
Break yarn and leave rem 8 (10: 12: 14: 16: 20) sts on a 2nd holder.
Shape pocket front
With RS facing, rejoin yarn to 54 sts on first holder, cast on and K 5 sts, patt to end. 59 sts.
Row 66 (WS): Patt to last 5 sts, K5.

Row 67: K5, patt to end.
These 2 rows set the sts - pocket opening edge 5 sts in g st with all other sts in patt.
Work 5 rows, ending with a WS row.
Row 73: Patt 6 sts, C8B, P1, C8F, patt 36 sts.
Work 15 rows, ending with a WS row.
Row 89: As row 73.
Work 13 rows, ending with a WS row.
Row 103: Patt 6 sts, slip next 4 sts onto cn and leave at back of work, K2, K2tog, then K2tog, K2 across 4 sts on cn, P1, slip next 4 sts onto cn and leave at front of work, K2, K2tog, then K2tog, K2 across 4 sts on cn, patt 36 sts. 55 sts.
Now working 6 sts in each cable panel instead of 8 sts, work 2 rows, ending with a **RS** row.
Join sections
Row 106 (WS): Patt across first 50 sts on needle, now holding RS of side front against WS of pocket front, K tog first st of side front with next st of pocket front, (K tog next st of side front with next st of pocket front) 4 times, patt rem 3 (5: 7: 9: 11: 15) sts of side front. 58 (60: 62: 64: 66: 70) sts.
Work 8 rows, ending with a WS row.
Row 115: Patt 9 (11: 13: 15: 17: 21) sts, C6B, P1, C6F, patt 36 sts.
Work 11 rows.
Last 12 rows form patt for rest of left front.
Cont in patt, inc 1 st at beg of 11th and foll 16th row, taking inc sts into patt. 60 (62: 64: 66: 68: 72) sts.
Cont straight until left front matches back to beg of armhole shaping, ending with a WS row.
Shape armhole
Keeping patt correct, cast off 3 (3: 4: 4: 5: 6) sts at beg of next row. 57 (59: 60: 62: 63: 66) sts.
Work 1 row.
Dec 1 st at armhole edge of next 3 (3: 3: 5: 5: 7) rows, then on foll 2 (3: 3: 2: 2: 2) alt rows, then on foll 4th row. 51 (52: 53: 54: 55: 56) sts.
Cont straight until 21 (21: 21: 23: 23: 23) rows less have been worked than on back to beg of shoulder shaping, ending with a **RS** row.
Shape neck
Keeping patt correct, cast off 20 sts at beg of next row. 31 (32: 33: 34: 35: 36) sts.
Dec 1 st at neck edge of next 5 rows, then on foll 5 (5: 5: 6: 6: 6) alt rows, then on foll 4th row.
20 (21: 22: 22: 23: 24) sts.
Work 1 row, ending with a WS row.
Shape shoulder
Cast off 7 (7: 7: 7: 8: 8) sts at beg of next and foll alt row.
Work 1 row.
Cast off rem 6 (7: 8: 8: 7: 8) sts.

Mark positions for 5 pairs of buttons along left front opening edge - first pair of buttons to come in row 69, top pair of buttons to come 3 cm below neck shaping, and rem 3 pairs of buttons evenly spaced between.

RIGHT FRONT
Cast on 68 (70: 72: 74: 76: 80) sts using 5mm (US 8) needles.
Row 1 (RS): K4, (P1, K1 tbl) 16 times, (K2, inc in next st, K1) twice, P1, (K1, inc in next st, K2) twice, (K1 tbl, P1) 7 (8: 9: 10: 11: 13) times, P1. 72 (74: 76: 78: 80: 84) sts.
Row 2: K15 (17: 19: 21: 23: 27), P10, K1, P10, K36.
Row 3: K4, (P1, K1 tbl) 16 times, K10, P1, K10, (K1 tbl, P1) 7 (8: 9: 10: 11: 13) times, P1.
Last 2 rows set the sts.
Cont as now set for a further 15 rows, ending with a WS row.
Row 19 (RS): Patt 36 sts, C10B, P1, C10F, patt 15 (17: 19: 21: 23: 27) sts.
Work 19 rows, dec 1 st at end of 8th of these rows and ending with a WS row.
71 (73: 75: 77: 79: 83) sts.
Row 39: Patt 36 sts, C10B, P1, C10F, patt 14 (16: 18: 20: 22: 26) sts.
Work 17 rows, dec 1 st at end of 2nd and foll 14th row and ending with a WS row.
69 (71: 73: 75: 77: 81) sts.
Row 57: Patt 36 sts, slip next 5 sts onto cn and leave at back of work, K3, K2tog, then K2tog, K3 across 5 sts on cn, P1, slip next 5 sts onto cn and leave at front of work, K3, K2tog, then K2tog, K3 across 5 sts on cn, patt 12 (14: 16: 18: 20: 24) sts.
65 (67: 69: 71: 73: 77) sts.
Now working 8 sts in each cable panel instead of 10 sts, work 7 rows, ending with a WS row.
Place pocket
Row 65 (RS): Patt 54 sts and turn, leaving rem 11 (13: 15: 17: 19: 23) sts on a holder.
Row 66: Cast on and K 5 sts, patt to end. 59 sts.
Row 67: Patt to last 5 sts, K5.
Row 68: K5, patt to end.
Last 2 rows set the sts - pocket opening edge 5 sts in g st with all other sts in patt.
Row 69 (buttonhole row) (RS): K3, K2tog tbl, (yfwd) twice, K2tog (to make first buttonhole of first pair - work twice into double yfwd on next row), patt 17 sts, K2tog tbl, (yfwd) twice, K2tog (to make 2nd buttonhole of first pair - work twice into double yfwd on next row), patt to end.

Working a further 4 pairs of buttonholes in this way to correspond with positions marked for buttons on left front and noting that no further reference will be made to buttonholes, cont as folls:

Work 3 rows, ending with a WS row.

Row 73: Patt 36 sts, C8B, P1, C8F, patt 6 sts.

Work 15 rows, ending with a WS row.

Row 89: As row 73.

Work 13 rows, ending with a WS row.

Row 103: Patt 36 sts, slip next 4 sts onto cn and leave at back of work, K2, K2tog, then K2tog, K2 across 4 sts on cn, P1, slip next 4 sts onto cn and leave at front of work, K2, K2tog, then K2tog, K2 across 4 sts on cn, patt 6 sts. 55 sts. Now working 6 sts in each cable panel instead of 8 sts, work 2 rows, ending with a **RS** row. Break yarn and leave sts on a 2nd holder.

Shape side front

With RS facing, K across 18 sts of second pocket lining, then patt across 11 (13: 15: 17: 19: 23) sts on first holder. 29 (31: 33: 35: 37: 41) sts. Keeping pocket lining sts in st st and side front sts in patt as set, dec 1 st at end of 4th and 2 foll 14th rows.

26 (28: 30: 32: 34: 38) sts.

Work a further 7 rows, ending with a WS row.

Row 105 (RS): Cast off 18 sts, patt to end. 8 (10: 12: 14: 16: 20) sts.

Join sections

Row 106 (WS): Patt across first 3 (5: 7: 9: 11: 15) sts on needle, now holding RS of side front against WS of pocket front, K tog next st of side front with first st of pocket front, (K tog next st of side front with next st of pocket front) 4 times, patt rem 50 sts of pocket front. 58 (60: 62: 64: 66: 70) sts.

Work 8 rows, ending with a WS row.

Row 115: Patt 36 sts, C6B, P1, C6F, patt 9 (11: 13: 15: 17: 21) sts.

Work 11 rows.

Last 12 rows form patt for rest of right front. Complete to match left front, reversing shapings.

SLEEVES (both alike)

Cast on 41 (43: 45: 47: 49: 51) sts using 5mm (US 8) needles.

Row 1 (RS): P1, *K1 tbl, P1, rep from * to end.

Row 2: Knit.

These 2 rows form patt.

Cont in patt, shaping sides by inc 1 st at each end of 13th (13th: 13th: 13th: 11th: 9th) and every foll 16th (16th: 16th: 18th: 14th: 14th) row to 51 (51: 51: 59: 53: 67) sts, then on every foll 18th (18th: 18th: -: 16th: -) row until there are 53 (55: 57: -: 63: -) sts, taking inc sts into patt.

Cont straight until sleeve measures 45 (46: 47: 48: 49: 50) cm, ending with a WS row.

Shape top

Keeping patt correct, cast off 3 (3: 4: 4: 5: 6) sts at beg of next 2 rows.

47 (49: 49: 51: 53: 55) sts.

Dec 1 st at each end of next 3 rows, then on foll alt row, then on 5 foll 4th rows.

29 (31: 31: 33: 35: 37) sts.

Work 1 row, ending with a WS row.

Dec 1 st at each end of next and every foll alt row to 25 sts, then on foll 3 rows, ending with a WS row.

Cast off rem 19 sts.

MAKING UP

Press all pieces with a warm iron over a damp cloth.

Join both shoulder seams using back stitch or mattress stitch if preferred.

Collar

Cast on 83 (83: 83: 89: 89: 89) sts using 4mm (US 6) needles.

Row 1 (RS): K1, *P1, K1, rep from * to end.

Row 2: As row 1.

These 2 rows form moss st.

Work in moss st for a further 10 rows, ending with a WS row.

Row 13 (RS): K1, P1, K3tog, moss st to last 5 sts, K3tog tbl, P1, K1.

79 (79: 79: 85: 85: 85) sts.

Work 11 rows.

Row 25: As row 13.

75 (75: 75: 81: 81: 81) sts.

Work 15 rows, ending with a WS row.

Cast off 12 (12: 12: 13: 13: 13) sts at beg of next 4 rows.

Cast off rem 27 (27: 27: 29: 29: 29) sts. Positioning row-end edges of collar 19 sts in from front opening edges, sew shaped cast-off edge of collar to neck edge.

Sleeve and shoulder tabs (make 4)

Cast on 7 sts using 4mm (US 6) needles.

Work in g st for 68 (70: 72: 74: 76: 78) rows, ending with a WS row.

Cast off.

Shoulder tab loops (make 2)

Cast on 10 sts using 4½mm (US 7) needles.

Cast off.

Join side seams. Join sleeve seams, enclosing one end of a tab in seam and positioning this tab 6 cm up from cast-on edge. Sew sleeves into armholes. Sew pocket linings in place on inside, then neatly sew down cast-on edge of pocket band. Using photograph as a guide, sew ends of shoulder tab loops to shoulders so that loop lays just next to armhole seam.

Sew on buttons as folls: Attach 10 buttons to left front to match buttonholes in right front. Secure ends of sleeve tabs by attaching a button through both layers. Thread shoulder tabs through shoulder tab loops and fold in half. Secure ends of tabs to shoulder seams by attaching a button through all layers. At top of front opening edges, make a button loop and attach small buttons to correspond with these button loops.

Belt

Cast on 10 sts using 4mm (US 6) needles. Work in g st for 130 (135: 140: 145: 150: 155) cm, ending with a WS row. Cast off. Thread buckle onto one end of belt and secure in place. Make belt loops to lay over side seams at waist position by making a short length of chain. Thread belt through belt loops. Insert shoulder pads if required.

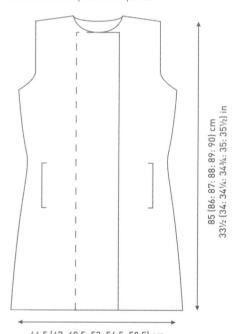

85 (86: 87: 88: 89: 90) cm
33½ (34: 34¼: 34¾: 35: 35½) in

44.5 (47: 49.5: 52: 54.5: 58.5) cm
17½ (18½: 19½: 20½: 21½: 23) in

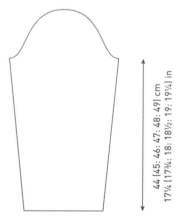

44 (45: 46: 47: 48: 49) cm
17¼ (17¾: 18: 18½: 19: 19¼) in

WISDOM

Recommendation
Suitable for the knitter with a little experience
Please see pages 36, 37 & 38 for photographs.

	XS	S	M	L	XL	XXL	
To fit	81	86	91	97	102	109	cm
bust	32	34	36	38	40	43	in

Rowan Felted Tweed
Main colour

	5	6	6	7	7	8	x 50gm

Contrast colour

	1	1	1	1	1	1	x 50gm

Photographed in Duck Egg trimmed with Carbon

Needles
1 pair 3mm (no 11) (US 2/3) needles
1 pair 3¼mm (no 10) (US 3) needles
1 pair 3¾mm (no 9) (US 5) needles

Buttons – 9

Tension
23 sts and 32 rows to 10 cm measured over stocking stitch, 25 sts and 34 rows to 10 cm measured over double moss stitch, both using 3¾mm (US 5) needles.

Shaping note: When working side and sleeve seam shaping within double moss st sections of patt, work increases and decreases on edge sts of rows. When decreasing during st st sections, work dec at beg of rows as "K2, K2tog" and at ends of rows as "K2tog tbl, K2". When increasing during st st sections, work inc at beg of rows as "K2, M1" and at ends of rows as "M1, K2".

BACK
Cast on 95 (101: 107: 113: 119: 129) sts using 3¼mm (US 3) needles and main colour.
Row 1 (RS): P0 (1: 0: 1: 0: 1), *K1, P1, rep from * to last 1 (0: 1: 0: 1: 0) st, K1 (0: 1: 0: 1: 0).
Row 2: As row 1.
Rows 3 and 4: K0 (1: 0: 1: 0: 1), *P1, K1, rep from * to last 1 (0: 1: 0: 1: 0) st, P1 (0: 1: 0: 1: 0).
These 4 rows form double moss st.
Cont in double moss st for a further 6 rows, ending with a WS row.
Change to 3¾mm (US 5) needles.
Cont in double moss st, shaping side seams (see shaping note above) by dec 1 st at each end of 5th and 3 foll 6th rows.
87 (93: 99: 105: 111: 121) sts.
Work 1 row, ending with a WS row.
Now work in patt as folls:
Beg with a K row, work in st st for 18 rows, dec 1 st at each end of 5th of these rows and ending with a WS row.
85 (91: 97: 103: 109: 119) sts.
Work in double moss st for 20 rows, inc 1 st at each end of 7th and foll 10th row, taking inc sts into patt and ending with a WS row.
89 (95: 101: 107: 113: 123) sts.
Last 38 rows form patt and cont side seam shaping.
Cont in patt, inc 1 st at each end of 7th and 3 foll 10th rows.
97 (103: 109: 115: 121: 131) sts.
Work 9 (9: 13: 13: 13: 13) rows, ending after 8 (8: 12: 12: 12: 12) rows in st st and with a WS row. (Back should measure approx 36 (36: 37: 37: 37: 37) cm.)

Shape armholes
Keeping patt correct, cast off 4 (5: 5: 6: 6: 7) sts at beg of next 2 rows.
89 (93: 99: 103: 109: 117) sts.
Dec 1 st at each end of next 5 (5: 7: 7: 9: 11) rows, then on foll 2 (3: 3: 4: 4: 4) alt rows, then on foll 4th row.
73 (75: 77: 79: 81: 85) sts.
Cont straight until armhole measures 18 (19: 19: 20: 21: 22) cm, ending with a WS row.
Shape back neck and shoulders
Cast off 7 (7: 7: 7: 7: 8) sts at beg of next 2 rows.
59 (61: 63: 65: 67: 69) sts.

Next row (RS): Cast off 7 (7: 7: 7: 7: 8) sts, patt until there are 10 (10: 11: 11: 12: 12) sts on right needle and turn, leaving rem sts on a holder.
Work each side of neck separately.
Cast off 4 sts at beg of next row.
Cast off rem 6 (6: 7: 7: 8: 8) sts.
With RS facing, rejoin yarn to rem sts, cast off centre 25 (27: 27: 29: 29: 29) sts, patt to end.
Complete to match first side, reversing shapings.

POCKET LININGS (make 2)
Cast on 25 (25: 27: 27: 29: 29) sts using 3¾mm (US 5) needles and contrast colour.
Beg with a K row, work in st st for 21 rows, ending with a **RS** row.
Break yarn and leave sts on a holder.

LEFT FRONT
Cast on 53 (56: 59: 62: 65: 70) sts using 3¼mm (US 3) needles and main colour.
Row 1 (RS): P0 (1: 0: 1: 0: 1), *K1, P1, rep from * to last st, K1.
Row 2: *K1, P1, rep from * to last 1 (0: 1: 0: 1: 0) st, K1 (0: 1: 0: 1: 0).
Row 3: K0 (1: 0: 1: 0: 1), *P1, K1, rep from * to last st, P1.
Row 4: *P1, K1, rep from * to last 1 (0: 1: 0: 1: 0) st, P1 (0: 1: 0: 1: 0).
These 4 rows form double moss st.
Cont in double moss st for a further 6 rows, ending with a WS row.
Change to 3¾mm (US 5) needles.
Cont in double moss st, shaping side seam by dec 1 st at beg of 5th and 3 foll 6th rows.
49 (52: 55: 58: 61: 66) sts.
Work 1 row, ending with a WS row.
Place pocket
Now working in patt as given for back, cont as folls:
Row 1 (RS): K9 (10: 11: 12: 13: 14), cast off next 25 (25: 27: 27: 29: 29) sts in double moss st, K to end.
Row 2: K3, P12 (14: 14: 16: 16: 20), with WS facing P across 25 (25: 27: 27: 29: 29) sts of first pocket lining, P to end.
These 2 rows place pocket and set position of g st front opening edge border.

Keeping sts correct as now set, work a further 16 rows, dec 1 st at beg of 3rd of these rows and ending with a WS row.
48 (51: 54: 57: 60: 65) sts.
Work in double moss st across **all** sts (including front opening edge sts) for 20 rows, inc 1 st at beg of 7th and foll 10th row, taking inc sts into patt and ending with a WS row.
50 (53: 56: 59: 62: 67) sts.
Last 38 rows form patt and cont side seam shaping.
Cont in patt, inc 1 st at beg of 7th and 3 foll 10th rows. 54 (57: 60: 63: 66: 71) sts.
Work 9 (9: 13: 13: 13: 13) rows, ending after 8 (8: 12: 12: 12: 12) rows in st st and with a WS row.

Shape armhole
Keeping patt correct, cast off 4 (5: 5: 6: 6: 7) sts at beg of next row.
50 (52: 55: 57: 60: 64) sts.
Work 1 row.
Dec 1 st at armhole edge of next 5 (5: 7: 7: 9: 11) rows, then on foll 2 (3: 3: 4: 4: 4) alt rows, then on foll 4th row.
42 (43: 44: 45: 46: 48) sts.
Cont straight until 18 (18: 18: 20: 20: 20) rows less have been worked than on back to beg of shoulder shaping, ending with a WS row.

Shape front neck
Next row (RS): Patt 30 (30: 31: 32: 33: 35) sts and turn, leaving rem 12 (13: 13: 13: 13: 13) sts on a holder.
Keeping patt correct, dec 1 st at neck edge of next 6 rows, then on foll 3 (3: 3: 4: 4: 4) alt rows, then on foll 4th row.
20 (20: 21: 21: 22: 24) sts.
Work 1 row, ending with a WS row.

Shape shoulder
Cast off 7 (7: 7: 7: 7: 8) sts at beg of next and foll alt row.
Work 1 row.
Cast off rem 6 (6: 7: 7: 8: 8) sts.
Mark positions for 9 buttons along left front opening edge - first button to come in row 25, top button to come just above neck shaping, and rem 7 buttons evenly spaced between.

RIGHT FRONT
Cast on 53 (56: 59: 62: 65: 70) sts using 3¼mm (US 3) needles and main colour.
Row 1 (RS): *K1, P1, rep from * to last 1 (0: 1: 0: 1: 0) st, K1 (0: 1: 0: 1: 0).
Row 2: P0 (1: 0: 1: 0: 1), *K1, P1, rep from * to last st, K1.
Row 3: *P1, K1, rep from * to last 1 (0: 1: 0: 1: 0) st, P1 (0: 1: 0: 1: 0).

Row 4: K0 (1: 0: 1: 0: 1), *P1, K1, rep from * to last st, P1.
These 4 rows form double moss st.
Cont in double moss st for a further 6 rows, ending with a WS row.
Change to 3¾mm (US 5) needles.
Cont in double moss st, shaping side seam by dec 1 st at end of 5th and foll 6th row.
51 (54: 57: 60: 63: 68) sts.
Work 3 rows, ending with a WS row.
Row 25 (buttonhole row) (RS): Patt 2 sts, work 2 tog tbl, yrn (to make a buttonhole), patt to end.
Working a further 7 buttonholes in this way to correspond with positions marked for buttons on left front and noting that no further reference will be made to buttonholes, cont as folls:
Dec 1 st at end of 2nd and foll 6th row.
49 (52: 55: 58: 61: 66) sts.
Work 1 row, ending with a WS row.

Place pocket
Now working in patt as given for back, cont as folls:
Row 1 (RS): K15 (17: 17: 19: 19: 23), cast off next 25 (25: 27: 27: 29: 29) sts in double moss, K to end.
Row 2: P9 (10: 11: 12: 13: 14), with WS facing P across 25 (25: 27: 27: 29: 29) sts of second pocket lining, P to last 3 sts, K3.
These 2 rows place pocket and set position of g st front opening edge border.
Keeping sts correct as now set, work a further 16 rows, dec 1 st at end of 3rd of these rows and ending with a WS row.
48 (51: 54: 57: 60: 65) sts.
Work in double moss st across **all** sts (including front opening edge sts) for 20 rows, inc 1 st at end of 7th and foll 10th row, taking inc sts into patt and ending with a WS row.
50 (53: 56: 59: 62: 67) sts.
Last 38 rows form patt and cont side seam shaping.
Complete to match left front, reversing shapings and working first row of neck shaping as folls:

Shape front neck
Next row (RS): Patt 12 (13: 13: 13: 13: 13) sts and slip these sts onto a holder, patt to end. 30 (30: 31: 32: 33: 35) sts.

SLEEVES (both alike)
Cast on 57 (59: 59: 61: 63: 65) sts using 3¼mm (US 3) needles and contrast colour.
Break off contrast colour and join in main colour.
Row 1 (WS): Purl.
Now work in double moss st as folls:

Row 1 (RS): K1, *P1, K1, rep from * to end.
Row 2: As row 1.
Rows 3 and 4: P1, *K1, P1, rep from * to end.
These 4 rows form double moss st.
Cont in double moss st for a further 6 rows, ending with a WS row.
Change to 3¾mm (US 5) needles.
Cont in double moss st for a further 10 (14: 14: 16: 20: 24) rows, shaping sides by inc 1 st at each end of 7th and 0 (0: 0: 0: 0: 1) foll 12th row, taking inc sts into patt and ending with a WS row. 59 (61: 61: 63: 65: 69) sts.
Starting with 18 rows in st st, now work in patt as given for back, shaping sides by inc 1 st at each end of 9th (5th: 7th: 5th: next: 9th) and every foll 12th (14th: 14th: 14th: 14th: 14th) row to 65 (73: 71: 71: 69: 81) sts, then on every foll 14th (-: 16th: 16th: 16th: -) row until there are 71 (-: 73: 75: 77: -) sts, taking inc sts into patt.
Work 9 rows, ending after 8 (8: 12: 12: 12: 12) rows in st st and with a WS row.
(Sleeve should measure approx 32 (33: 34: 35: 36: 37) cm.)

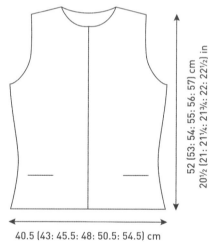

40.5 (43: 45.5: 48: 50.5: 54.5) cm
16 (17: 18: 19: 20: 21½) in

52 (53: 54: 55: 56: 57) cm
20½ (21: 21¼: 21¾: 22: 22½) in

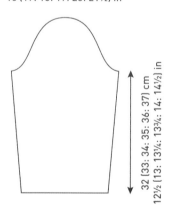

32 (33: 34: 35: 36: 37) cm
12½ (13: 13¼: 13¾: 14: 14½) in

Continued on next page...

RIVER

Recommendation
Suitable for the knitter with a little experience
Please see page 11 for photograph.

	XS	S	M	L	XL	XXL	
To fit	86	91	97	102	109	114	cm
hips	34	36	38	40	42	45	in

Rowan Lima

	4	4	5	5	6	6	x 50gm

Photographed in Peru

Needles
1 pair 4½mm (no 7) (US 7) needles

Extras – Waist length of 2.5 cm wide elastic

Tension
23 sts and 36 rows to 10 cm measured over
pattern when slightly stretched using 4½mm
(US 7) needles.

BACK and FRONT (both alike)
Cast on 79 (85: 91: 97: 103: 111) sts using
4½mm (US 7) needles.
Row 1 (RS): K1 (0: 3: 2: 1: 1), P1, *K3, P1, rep
from * to last 1 (0: 3: 2: 1: 1) sts, K1 (0: 3: 2: 1: 1).
Row 2: K3 (2: 1: 0: 3: 3), P1, *K3, P1, rep from
* to last 3 (2: 1: 0: 3: 3) sts, K3 (2: 1: 0: 3: 3).
These 2 rows form patt.
Cont in patt for a further 4 rows, ending with
a WS row.
Counting in from both ends of last row, place
markers after 13th (16th: 15th: 18th: 17th:
21st) sts in from both ends of row.
Next row (inc) (RS): Patt to marker, slip
marker onto right needle, M1, patt to next
marker, M1, slip marker onto right needle,
patt to end. 81 (87: 93: 99: 105: 113) sts.
Taking inc sts into patt as set by sts between
markers, work 5 rows.
Rep last 6 rows twice more, and then first
of these rows (the inc row) again.
87 (93: 99: 105: 111: 119) sts.
Cont straight until work measures 23 (23: 23: 25:
25: 27) cm, ending with RS facing for next row.
Shape waist darts
Counting in from both ends of last row, place
markers after 9th (12th: 11th: 14th: 13th:
17th) sts in from both ends of row, miss next
16 sts and then place another pair of markers.
(4 markers in total, with 37 (37: 45: 45:
53: 53) sts between centre markers.)
Next row (dec) (RS): Patt to first marker, slip
marker onto right needle, work 2 tog, patt to

next marker, slip marker onto right needle,
work 2 tog, *patt to within 2 sts of next marker,
work 2 tog tbl, slip marker onto right needle,
rep from * once more, patt to end.
83 (89: 95: 101: 107: 115) sts.
Keeping patt correct and working all decreases
as set by last row, dec 4 sts (1 st near each
marker) across 8th row, then on 2 foll 6th
rows, then on 3 foll 4th rows, then on foll
alt row. 55 (61: 67: 73: 79: 87) sts.
Work 1 row, ending with a WS row.
Cast off loosely in patt.

MAKING UP
Do NOT press.
Join side seams using back stitch or mattress
stitch if preferred. Join ends of elastic. Attach
elastic to inside of cast-off edge by working
a herringbone stitch casing over elastic.

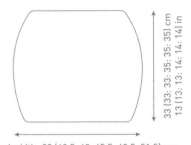

Actual width: 38 (40.5: 43: 45.5: 48.5: 51.5) cm
15 (16: 17: 18: 19: 20¼) in

To fit hips: 86 (91: 97: 102: 109: 114) cm
34 (36: 38: 40: 42: 45) in

Shape top
Keeping patt correct, cast off 4 (5: 5: 6: 6: 7)
sts at beg of next 2 rows.
63 (63: 63: 63: 65: 67) sts.
Dec 1 st at each end of next 3 rows, then
on foll alt row, then on 6 (7: 7: 8: 8: 8) foll
4th rows.
43 (41: 41: 39: 41: 43) sts.
Work 1 row, ending with a WS row.
Dec 1 st at each end of next and foll 3 (2: 2:
1: 2: 3) alt rows, then on foll 5 rows, ending
with a WS row. Cast off rem 25 sts.

MAKING UP
Press all pieces with a warm iron over a damp
cloth.
Join both shoulder seams using back stitch or
mattress stitch if preferred.
Neckband
With RS facing, using 3mm (US 2/3) needles
and main colour, slip 12 (13: 13: 13: 13: 13)
sts from right front holder onto right needle,
rejoin yarn and pick up and knit 21 (21: 21:
23: 23: 23) sts up right side of neck, 33 (35:
35: 37: 37: 37) sts from back, and 21 (21: 21:

23: 23: 23) sts down left side of neck, then
patt across 12 (13: 13: 13: 13: 13) sts on left
front holder. 99 (103: 103: 109: 109: 109) sts.
Work in g st for 1 row, ending with a WS row.
Row 2 (RS): K2, K2tog tbl, yfwd (to make 9th
buttonhole), K to end.
Work in g st for a further 6 rows, ending with
a **RS** row.
Cast off knitwise (on **WS**).
Sew pocket linings in place on inside. Join side
seams. Join sleeve seams. Sew sleeves into
armholes. Sew on buttons.

SKYLARK

LACE RIBBED CARDIGAN WITH SOFT NECKLINE

Recommendation

Suitable for the knitter with a little experience
Please see page 18 for photograph.

	XS	S	M	L	XL	XXL	
To fit	**81**	**86**	**91**	**97**	**102**	**109**	cm
bust	32	34	36	38	40	43	in

Rowan Lima

| | 10 | 11 | 12 | 12 | 13 | 14 | x 50gm |

Photographed in Argentina

Needles

1 pair 4½mm (no 7) (US 7) needles
1 pair 5½mm (no 5) (US 9) needles

Buttons – 11

Tension

24 sts and 28 rows to 10 cm measured over
pattern using 5½mm (US 9) needles.

BACK

Cast on 102 (108: 114: 120: 126: 136) sts
using 5½mm (US 9) needles.
Row 1 (RS): K1 (1: 1: 1: 1: 0), *P1, K2,
rep from * to last 2 (2: 2: 2: 2: 1) sts, P1,
K1 (1: 1: 1: 1: 0).
Row 2: P1 (1: 1: 1: 1: 0), *K1, P2, rep from
* to last 2 (2: 2: 2: 2: 1) sts, K1, P1 (1: 1: 1:
1: 0).
These 2 rows form rib.
Cont in rib for a further 8 rows, ending with
a WS row.
Now work in patt as folls:
Row 1 (RS): K1 (1: 1: 1: 1: 0), (P1, K2) 0 (1:
0: 1: 0: 0) times, *P1, K2tog, yfrn, P1, K2, rep
from * to last 5 (2: 5: 2: 5: 4) sts, (P1, K2tog,
yfrn) 1 (0: 1: 0: 1: 1) times, P1, K1 (1: 1: 1:
1: 0).
Row 2: P1 (1: 1: 1: 1: 0), *K1, P2, rep from
* to last 2 (2: 2: 2: 2: 1) sts, K1, P1 (1: 1: 1:
1: 0).
Row 3: K1 (1: 1: 1: 1: 0), (P1, K2) 0 (1: 0: 1:
0: 0) times, *P1, yon, K2tog tbl, P1, K2, rep
from * to last 5 (2: 5: 2: 5: 4) sts, (P1, yon,
K2tog tbl) 1 (0: 1: 0: 1: 1) times, P1, K1 (1: 1:
1: 1: 0).
Row 4: As row 2.
These 4 rows form patt.
Work in patt for a further 4 rows, ending with
a WS row.
Keeping patt correct, dec 1 st at each end
of next and 6 foll 4th rows.
88 (94: 100: 106: 112: 122) sts.
Work 17 rows, ending with a WS row.
Inc 1 st at each end of next and 4 foll 10th
rows, taking inc sts into patt.
98 (104: 110: 116: 122: 132) sts.
Cont straight until back measures
40 (40: 41: 41: 41: 41) cm, ending
with a WS row.
Shape armholes
Keeping patt correct, cast off 4 (5: 5: 6: 6: 7)
sts at beg of next 2 rows.
90 (94: 100: 104: 110: 118) sts.
Dec 1 st at each end of next 5 (5: 7: 7: 9: 11)
rows, then on foll 2 (3: 3: 4: 4: 5) alt rows,
then on foll 4th row.
74 (76: 78: 80: 82: 84) sts.
Cont straight until armhole measures 12 (13:
13: 14: 15: 16) cm, ending with a WS row.

Shape back neck
Next row (RS): Patt 15 (15: 16: 16: 17: 18)
sts and turn, leaving rem sts on a holder.
Work each side of neck separately.
Keeping patt correct, dec 1 st at neck edge
of next 4 rows, then on foll 2 alt rows, then
on foll 4th row.
8 (8: 9: 9: 10: 11) sts.
Work 1 row, ending with a WS row.
Shape shoulder
Cast off 4 (4: 4: 4: 5: 5) sts at beg of next row.
Work 1 row.
Cast off rem 4 (4: 5: 5: 5: 6) sts.
With RS facing, rejoin yarn to rem sts, cast off
centre 44 (46: 46: 48: 48: 48) sts, patt to end.
Complete to match first side, reversing
shapings.

LEFT FRONT

Cast on 58 (61: 64: 67: 70: 75) sts using
5½mm (US 9) needles.
Row 1 (RS): K1 (1: 1: 1: 1: 0), *P1, K2, rep
from * to last 6 sts, P6.
Row 2: K5, *K1, P2, rep from * to last 2 (2: 2:
2: 2: 1) sts, K1, P1 (1: 1: 1: 1: 0).
Row 3: K1 (1: 1: 1: 1: 0), *P1, K2, rep from *
to last 6 sts, P1, K5.
Row 4: P5, *K1, P2, rep from * to last 2 (2: 2:
2: 2: 1) sts, K1, P1 (1: 1: 1: 1: 0).
These 4 rows set the sts - front opening
edge 5 sts in ridge patt with all other sts
in rib.
Cont as set for a further 6 rows, ending
with a WS row.
Now work in patt as folls:
Row 1 (RS): K1 (1: 1: 1: 1: 0), (P1, K2) 0 (1:
0: 1: 0: 0) times, *P1, K2tog, yfrn, P1, K2, rep
from * to last 9 sts, P1, K2tog, yfrn, P1,
patt 5 sts.
Row 2: Patt 5 sts, *K1, P2, rep from * to last
2 (2: 2: 2: 2: 1) sts, K1, P1 (1: 1: 1: 1: 0).
Row 3: K1 (1: 1: 1: 1: 0), (P1, K2) 0 (1: 0: 1:
0: 0) times, *P1, yon, K2tog tbl, P1, K2, rep
from * to last 9 sts, P1, yon, K2tog tbl, P1,
patt 5 sts.
Row 4: As row 2.
These 4 rows form patt with front opening
edge 5 sts still in ridge patt.
Work in patt for a further 4 rows, ending
with a WS row.

Keeping patt correct, dec 1 st at beg of next and 6 foll 4th rows. 51 (54: 57: 60: 63: 68) sts.
Work 17 rows, ending with a WS row.
Inc 1 st at beg of next and 4 foll 10th rows, taking inc sts into patt.
56 (59: 62: 65: 68: 73) sts.
Cont straight until left front matches back to beg of armhole shaping, ending with a WS row.

Shape armhole
Keeping patt correct, cast off 4 (5: 5: 6: 6: 7) sts at beg of next row. 52 (54: 57: 59: 62: 66) sts.
Work 1 row.
Dec 1 st at armhole edge of next 5 (5: 7: 7: 9: 11) rows, then on foll 2 (3: 3: 4: 4: 5) alt rows, then on foll 4th row. 44 (45: 46: 47: 48: 49) sts.
Cont straight until 6 (6: 6: 8: 8: 8) rows less have been worked than on back to beg of back neck shaping, ending with a WS row. (**Note**: Back neck shaping is 14 rows below shoulder shaping.)

Shape front neck
Next row (RS): Patt 34 (34: 35: 36: 37: 38) sts and turn, leaving rem 10 (11: 11: 11: 11: 11) sts on a holder.
Keeping patt correct, cast off 14 sts at beg of next row. 20 (20: 21: 22: 23: 24) sts.
Dec 1 st at neck edge of next 9 rows, then on foll 2 (2: 2: 3: 3: 3) alt rows, then on foll 4th row. 8 (8: 9: 9: 10: 11) sts.
Work 1 row, ending with a WS row.

Shape shoulder
Cast off 4 (4: 4: 4: 5: 5) sts at beg of next row.
Work 1 row.
Cast off rem 4 (4: 5: 5: 5: 6) sts.
Mark positions for 10 buttons along left front opening edge - first button to come in row 3, top button to come just above neck shaping, and rem 8 buttons evenly spaced between.

RIGHT FRONT
Cast on 58 (61: 64: 67: 70: 75) sts using 5½mm (US 9) needles.
Row 1 (RS): P5, *P1, K2, rep from * to last 2 (2: 2: 2: 2: 1) sts, P1, K1 (1: 1: 1: 1: 0).
Row 2: P1 (1: 1: 1: 1: 0), *K1, P2, rep from * to last 6 sts, K6.
Row 3 (buttonhole row): K2, K2tog tbl, yfwd (to make a buttonhole), K1, *P1, K2, rep from * to last 2 (2: 2: 2: 2: 1) sts, P1, K1 (1: 1: 1: 1: 0).
Working a further 8 buttonholes in this way to correspond with positions marked for buttons on left front and noting that no further reference will be made to buttonholes, cont as folls:
Row 4: P1 (1: 1: 1: 1: 0), *K1, P2, rep from * to last 6 sts, K1, P5.
These 4 rows set the sts - front opening edge 5 sts in ridge patt with all other sts in rib.

Cont as set for a further 6 rows, ending with a WS row.
Now work in patt as folls:
Row 1 (RS): Patt 5 sts, *P1, K2tog, yfrn, P1, K2, rep from * to last 5 (2: 5: 2: 5: 4) sts, (P1, K2tog, yfrn) 1 (0: 1: 0: 1: 1) times, P1, K1 (1: 1: 1: 1: 0).
Row 2: P1 (1: 1: 1: 1: 0), *K1, P2, rep from * to last 6 sts, K1, patt 5 sts.
Row 3: Patt 5 sts, *P1, yon, K2tog tbl, P1, K2, rep from * to last 5 (2: 5: 2: 5: 4) sts, (P1, yon, K2tog tbl) 1 (0: 1: 0: 1: 1) times, P1, K1 (1: 1: 1: 1: 0).
Row 4: As row 2.
These 4 rows form patt with front opening edge 5 sts still in ridge patt.
Work in patt for a further 4 rows, ending with a WS row.
Keeping patt correct, dec 1 st at end of next and 6 foll 4th rows. 51 (54: 57: 60: 63: 68) sts.
Complete to match left front, reversing shapings and working first row of neck shaping as folls:

Shape front neck
Next row (RS): Patt 10 (11: 11: 11: 11: 11) sts and slip these sts onto a holder, cast off next 14 sts, patt to end.
20 (20: 21: 22: 23: 24) sts.

SLEEVES (both alike)
Cast on 44 (46: 46: 48: 50: 52) sts using 5½mm (US 9) needles.
Row 1 (RS): K2 (0: 0: 1: 2: 0), *P1, K2, rep from * to last 0 (1: 1: 2: 0: 1) sts, P0 (1: 1: 1: 0: 1), K0 (0: 0: 1: 0: 0).
Row 2: P2 (0: 0: 1: 2: 0), *K1, P2, rep from * to last 0 (1: 1: 2: 0: 1) sts, K0 (1: 1: 1: 0: 1), P0 (0: 0: 1: 0: 0).
These 2 rows form rib.
Cont in rib for a further 22 rows, inc 1 st at each end of 15th of these rows and ending with a WS row. 46 (48: 48: 50: 52: 54) sts.
Now work in patt as folls:
Row 1 (RS): Inc in first st, P0 (0: 0: 0: 0: 1), K0 (0: 0: 1: 2: 2), P0 (1: 1: 1: 1: 1), *yon, K2tog tbl, P1, K2, P1, rep from * to last 3 (4: 4: 5: 6: 1) sts, (yon, K2tog tbl) 1 (1: 1: 1: 1: 0) times, P0 (1: 1: 1: 1: 0), K0 (0: 0: 1: 2: 0), inc in last st. 48 (50: 50: 52: 54: 56) sts.
Row 2: P1 (2: 2: 0: 1: 2), *K1, P2, rep from * to last 2 (0: 0: 1: 2: 0) sts, K1 (0: 0: 1: 1: 0), P1 (0: 0: 0: 1: 0).
Row 3: K0 (0: 0: 0: 1: 2), P0 (0: 0: 1: 1: 1), K1 (2: 2: 2: 2: 2), P1, *K2tog, yfrn, P1, K2, P1, rep from * to last 4 (5: 5: 0: 1: 2) sts, (K2tog, yfrn, P1) 1 (1: 1: 0: 0: 0) times, K1 (2: 2: 0: 1: 2).
Row 4: As row 2.

These 4 rows form patt and cont sleeve shaping.
Cont in patt, shaping sides by inc 1 st at each end of 5th and every foll 8th row to 70 (70: 66: 66: 64: 64) sts, then on every foll - (10th: 10th: 10th: 10th: 10th) row until there are - (72: 72: 74: 76: 78) sts, taking inc sts into patt.
Cont straight until sleeve measures 45 (46: 47: 48: 49: 50) cm, ending with a WS row.

Shape top
Keeping patt correct, cast off 4 (5: 5: 6: 6: 7) sts at beg of next 2 rows.
62 (62: 62: 62: 64: 64) sts.
Dec 1 st at each end of next 3 rows, then on foll alt row, then on 3 (4: 4: 5: 5: 6) foll 4th rows. 48 (46: 46: 44: 46: 44) sts.
Work 1 row, ending with a WS row.
Dec 1 st at each end of next and foll 4 (3: 3: 2: 3: 2) alt rows, then on foll 5 rows, ending with a WS row. Cast off rem 28 sts.

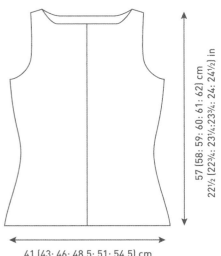

57 (58: 59: 60: 61: 62) cm
22½ (22¾: 23¼: 23¾: 24: 24½) in

41 (43: 46: 48.5: 51: 54.5) cm
16 (17: 18: 19: 20: 21½) in

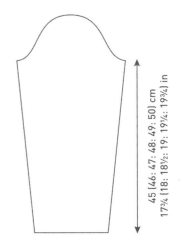

45 (46: 47: 48: 49: 50) cm
17¾ (18: 18½: 19: 19¼: 19¾) in

Continued on next page...

Recommendation

Suitable for the knitter with a little experience
Please see pages 12 & 13 for photographs.

	XS	S	M	L	XL	XXL	
To fit	**81**	**86**	**91**	**97**	**102**	**109**	cm
bust	32	34	36	38	40	43	in

Rowan Big Wool

	5	5	6	6	7	8	x 100gm

Photographed in Concrete

Needles

1 pair 9mm (no 00) (US 13) needles
1 pair 10mm (no 000) (US 15) needles

Tension

10 sts and 15 rows to 10 cm measured over
pattern using 10mm (US 15) needles.

Pattern note: The number of sts varies whilst
working patt. All st counts given presume there
are 8 sts between markers at all times.

PAGE
SHORT SLEEVED EDGE TO EDGE JACKET

BACK

Cast on 39 (41: 43: 47: 49: 53) sts using
10mm (US 15) needles.
Row 1 (WS): K5 (6: 7: 9: 10: 12), place marker
on right needle, K8, place marker on right needle,
K13, place marker on right needle, K8, place
marker on right needle, K5 (6: 7: 9: 10: 12).
Now work in patt as folls:
Row 1 (RS): *K to marker, slip marker onto
right needle, yfwd, K8, yfwd, slip marker onto
right needle, rep from * once more, K to end.
Row 2: K2 (0: 0: 2: 0: 1), P1 (0: 1: 1: 0:
1), (K3, P1) 0 (1: 1: 1: 2: 2) times, K2, *slip
marker onto right needle, K1, P8, K1, slip
marker onto right needle*, K2, (P1, K3) twice,
P1, K2, rep from * to * once more, K2, (P1, K3)
0 (1: 1: 1: 2: 2) times, P1 (0: 1: 1: 0: 1), K2 (0:
0: 2: 0: 1).
Row 3: *K to marker, slip marker onto right
needle, K1, yfwd, K8, yfwd, K1, slip marker
onto right needle, rep from * once more,
K to end.
Row 4: K0 (1: 2: 0: 1: 0), P1 (1: 1: 1: 1: 0),
(K3, P1) 1 (1: 1: 2: 2: 3) times, *slip marker
onto right needle, K2, P8, K2, slip marker onto
right needle*, (P1, K3) 3 times, P1, rep from *
to * once more, (P1, K3) 1 (1: 1: 2: 2: 3) times,
P1 (1: 1: 1: 1: 0), K0 (1: 2: 0: 1: 0).
Row 5: *K to marker, slip marker onto right
needle, K2, yfwd, K8, yfwd, K2, slip marker onto
right needle, rep from * once more, K to end.

Row 6: K2 (0: 0: 2: 0: 1), P1 (0: 1: 1:
0: 1), (K3, P1) 0 (1: 1: 1: 2: 2) times,
K2, *slip marker onto right needle, K1,
P1, K1, P8, K1, P1, K1, slip marker onto
right needle*, K2, (P1, K3) twice, P1, K2,
rep from * to * once more, K2, (P1, K3)
0 (1: 1: 1: 2: 2) times, P1 (0: 1: 1: 0: 1),
K2 (0: 0: 2: 0: 1).
Row 7: *K to marker, slip marker onto right
needle, K3, K4tog tbl, K4tog, K3, slip marker
onto right needle, rep from * once more,
K to end.
Row 8: K0 (1: 2: 0: 1: 0), P1 (1: 1: 1: 1:
0), (K3, P1) 1 (1: 1: 2: 2: 3) times, *slip
marker onto right needle, K8, slip marker
onto right needle*, (P1, K3) 3 times, P1,
rep from * to * once more, (P1, K3) 1 (1: 1:
2: 2: 3) times, P1 (1: 1: 1: 1: 0), K0 (1: 2:
0: 1: 0).
These 8 rows form patt.
Cont in patt, shaping side seams by dec
1 st at each end of 3rd and foll 8th row.
35 (37: 39: 43: 45: 49) sts.
Work 11 rows, ending with a WS row.
Inc 1 st at each end of next and foll 12th row,
taking inc sts into patt.
39 (41: 43: 47: 49: 53) sts.
Work 7 (7: 9: 9: 9: 9) rows, ending with
a WS row.
(Back should measure 34 (34: 35: 35:
35: 35) cm.)

SKYLARK – Continued from previous page.

MAKING UP

Press all pieces with a warm iron over a damp
cloth.
Join both shoulder seams using back stitch or
mattress stitch if preferred.
Neckband
With RS facing and using 4½mm (US 7)
needles, slip 10 (11: 11: 11: 11: 11) sts from
right front holder onto right needle, rejoin yarn
and pick up and knit 33 (33: 33: 35: 35: 35)

sts up right side of front neck, 14 sts down right
side of back neck, 44 (45: 45: 47: 47: 47) sts
from back, 14 sts up left side of back neck, and
33 (33: 33: 35: 35: 35) sts down left side of
front neck, then patt across 10 (11: 11: 11: 11:
11) sts on left front holder.
158 (161: 161: 167: 167: 167) sts.
Row 1 (WS): Patt 5 sts, K1, *P2, K1, rep from *
to last 5 sts, patt 5 sts.
This row sets the sts - front opening edge 5 sts

(at both ends of rows) still in ridge patt and
rem sts in rib.
Making 10th buttonhole in next row and 11th
buttonhole in foll 8th row, cont as set for a
further 11 rows, ending with a **RS** row.
Cast off in patt (on **WS**).
Join side seams.
Join sleeve seams.
Sew sleeves into armholes.
Sew on buttons.

Shape armholes
Keeping patt correct, cast off 3 sts at beg of next 2 rows.
33 (35: 37: 41: 43: 47) sts.
Dec 1 st at each end of next 1 (2: 2: 4: 4: 6) rows.
31 (31: 33: 33: 35: 35) sts.
Work 19 (18: 16: 14: 14: 20) rows, ending after patt row 8 and with a WS row.
Now working sts between markers in st st, not patt, cont as folls:
Work 0 (2: 4: 4: 6: 0) rows, ending with a WS row.

Shape back neck and shoulders
Next row (RS): Cast off 4 (4: 5: 4: 5: 5) sts, patt until there are 5 sts on right needle and turn, leaving rem sts on a holder.
Work each side of neck separately.
Work 1 row.
Cast off rem 5 sts.
With RS facing, rejoin yarn to rem sts, cast off centre 13 (13: 13: 15: 15: 15) sts, patt to end.
Complete to match first side, reversing shapings.

LEFT FRONT
Cast on 23 (24: 25: 27: 28: 30) sts using 10mm (US 15) needles.
Row 1 (WS): K10, place marker on right needle, K8, place marker on right needle, K5 (6: 7: 9: 10: 12).
Now work in patt as folls:
Row 1 (RS): K to marker, slip marker onto right needle, yfwd, K8, yfwd, slip marker onto right needle, K to end.
Row 2: (K3, P1) twice, K2, slip marker onto right needle, K1, P8, K1, slip marker onto right needle, K2, (P1, K3) 0 (1: 1: 1: 2: 2) times, P1 (0: 1: 1: 0: 1), K2 (0: 0: 2: 0: 1).
Row 3: K to marker, slip marker onto right needle, K1, yfwd, K8, yfwd, K1, slip marker onto right needle, K to end.
Row 4: K5, P1, K3, P1, slip marker onto right needle, K2, P8, K2, slip marker onto right needle, (P1, K3) 1 (1: 1: 2: 2: 3) times, P1 (1: 1: 1: 1: 0), K0 (1: 2: 0: 1: 0).
Row 5: K to marker, slip marker onto right needle, K2, yfwd, K8, yfwd, K2, slip marker onto right needle, K to end.
Row 6: (K3, P1) twice, K2, slip marker onto right needle, K1, P1, K1, P8, K1, P1, K1, slip marker onto right needle, K2, (P1, K3) 0 (1: 1: 1: 2: 2) times, P1 (0: 1: 1: 0: 1), K2 (0: 0: 2: 0: 1).
Row 7: K to marker, slip marker onto right needle, K3, K4tog tbl, K4tog, K3, slip marker onto right needle, K to end.

Row 8: K5, P1, K3, P1, slip marker onto right needle, K8, slip marker onto right needle, (P1, K3) 1 (1: 1: 2: 2: 3) times, P1 (1: 1: 1: 1: 0), K0 (1: 2: 0: 1: 0).
These 8 rows form patt.
Cont in patt, shaping side seam by dec 1 st at beg of 3rd and foll 8th row.
21 (22: 23: 25: 26: 28) sts.
Work 11 rows, ending with a WS row.
Inc 1 st at beg of next and foll 12th row, taking inc sts into patt.
23 (24: 25: 27: 28: 30) sts.
Work 7 (7: 9: 9: 9: 9) rows, ending with a WS row.
Shape armhole
Keeping patt correct, cast off 3 sts at beg of next row.
20 (21: 22: 24: 25: 27) sts.
Work 1 row.
Dec 1 st at armhole edge of next 1 (2: 2: 4: 4: 6) rows.
19 (19: 20: 20: 21: 21) sts.
Keeping sts between markers correct as set by back (by working last 0 (2: 4: 4: 6: 0) rows before shoulder in st st), cont as folls:
Work 9 (10: 10: 6: 8: 8) rows, ending with a WS row.
Shape front neck
Next row (RS): Patt to last 6 sts and turn, leaving rem 6 sts on a holder.
13 (13: 14: 14: 15: 15) sts.
Keeping patt correct, dec 1 st at neck edge of next 2 rows, then on 2 (2: 2: 3: 3: 3) alt rows. 9 (9: 10: 9: 10: 10) sts.
Work 3 rows, ending with a WS row.
Shape shoulder
Cast off 4 (4: 5: 4: 5: 5) sts at beg of next row.
Work 1 row.
Cast off rem 5 sts.

RIGHT FRONT
Cast on 23 (24: 25: 27: 28: 30) sts using 10mm (US 15) needles.
Row 1 (WS): K5 (6: 7: 9: 10: 12), place marker on right needle, K8, place marker on right needle, K10.
Now work in patt as folls:
Row 1 (RS): K to marker, slip marker onto right needle, yfwd, K8, yfwd, slip marker onto right needle, K to end.
Row 2: K2 (0: 0: 2: 0: 1), P1 (0: 1: 1: 0: 1), (K3, P1) 0 (1: 1: 1: 2: 2) times, K2, slip marker onto right needle, K1, P8, K1, slip marker onto right needle, K2, (P1, K3) twice.
Row 3: K to marker, slip marker onto right needle, K1, yfwd, K8, yfwd, K1, slip marker onto right needle, K to end.

Row 4: K0 (1: 2: 0: 1: 0), P1 (1: 1: 1: 1: 0), (K3, P1) 1 (1: 1: 2: 2: 3) times, slip marker onto right needle, K2, P8, K2, slip marker onto right needle, P1, K3, P1, K5.
Row 5: K to marker, slip marker onto right needle, K2, yfwd, K8, yfwd, K2, slip marker onto right needle, K to end.
Row 6: K2 (0: 0: 2: 0: 1), P1 (0: 1: 1: 0: 1), (K3, P1) 0 (1: 1: 1: 2: 2) times, K2, slip marker onto right needle, K1, P1, K1, P8, K1, P1, K1, slip marker onto right needle, K2, (P1, K3) twice.
Row 7: K to marker, slip marker onto right needle, K3, K4tog tbl, K4tog, K3, slip marker onto right needle, K to end.
Row 8: K0 (1: 2: 0: 1: 0), P1 (1: 1: 1: 1: 0), (K3, P1) 1 (1: 1: 2: 2: 3) times, slip marker onto right needle, K8, slip marker onto right needle, P1, K3, P1, K5.
These 8 rows form patt.
Cont in patt, shaping side seam by dec 1st at end of 3rd and foll 8th row.
21 (22: 23: 25: 26: 28) sts.
Complete to match left front, reversing shapings and working first row of neck shaping as folls:
Shape front neck
Next row (RS): Patt 6 sts and slip these sts onto a holder, patt to end.
13 (13: 14: 14: 15: 15) sts.

SLEEVES (both alike)
Cast on 28 (28: 30: 30: 32: 32) sts using 10mm (US 15) needles.
Row 1 (WS): K10 (10: 11: 11: 12: 12), place marker on right needle, K8, place marker on right needle, K10 (10: 11: 11: 12: 12).
Now work in patt as folls:
Row 1 (RS): K to marker, slip marker onto right needle, yfwd, K8, yfwd, slip marker onto right needle, K to end.
Row 2: K0 (0: 0: 0: 1: 1), P0 (0: 1: 1: 1: 1), (K3, P1) twice, K2, slip marker onto right needle, K1, P8, K1, slip marker onto right needle, K2, (P1, K3) twice, P0 (0: 1: 1: 1: 1), K0 (0: 0: 0: 1: 1).
Row 3: K to marker, slip marker onto right needle, K1, yfwd, K8, yfwd, K1, slip marker onto right needle, K to end.
Row 4: K1 (1: 2: 2: 0: 0), P1 (1: 1: 1: 0: 0), (K3, P1) 2 (2: 2: 2: 3: 3) times, slip marker onto right needle, K2, P8, K2, slip marker onto right needle, (P1, K3) 2 (2: 2: 2: 3: 3) times, P1 (1: 1: 1: 0: 0), K1 (1: 2: 2: 0: 0).
Row 5: K to marker, slip marker onto right needle, K2, yfwd, K8, yfwd, K2, slip marker onto right needle, K to end.

Row 6: K0 (0: 0: 0: 1: 1), P0 (0: 1: 1: 1: 1), (K3, P1) twice, K2, slip marker onto right needle, K1, P1, K1, P8, K1, P1, K1, slip marker onto right needle, K2, (P1, K3) twice, P0 (0: 1: 1: 1: 1), K0 (0: 0: 0: 1: 1).

Row 7: K to marker, slip marker onto right needle, K3, K4tog tbl, K4tog, K3, slip marker onto right needle, K to end.

Row 8: K1 (1: 2: 2: 0: 0), P1 (1: 1: 1: 0: 0), (K3, P1) 2 (2: 2: 2: 3: 3) times, slip marker onto right needle, K8, slip marker onto right needle, (P1, K3) 2 (2: 2: 2: 3: 3) times, P1 (1: 1: 1: 0: 0), K1 (1: 2: 2: 0: 0).

These 8 rows form patt.

Shape top

Keeping patt correct, cast off 3 sts at beg of next 2 rows. 22 (22: 24: 24: 26: 26) sts.

(**Note**: After 3rd rep of patt row 8, work sts between markers in st st.)

Dec 1 st at each end of next and 2 foll 4th rows, then on foll 2 (2: 3: 3: 4: 4) alt rows, then on foll 2 rows, ending with a **RS** row.

Cast off rem 8 sts (on **WS**).

MAKING UP

Press all pieces with a warm iron over a damp cloth.

Join both shoulder seams using back stitch or mattress stitch if preferred.

Neckband

With RS facing and using 9mm (US 13) needles, slip 6 sts from right front holder onto right needle, rejoin yarn and pick up and knit 12 (12: 12: 13: 13: 13) sts up right side of neck, 15 (15: 15: 17: 17: 17) sts from back, and 12 (12: 12: 13: 13: 13) sts down left side of neck, then K across 6 sts on left front holder. 51 (51: 51: 55: 55: 55) sts.

Cast off knitwise (on **WS**).

Join side seams. Join sleeve seams.

Sew sleeves into armholes.

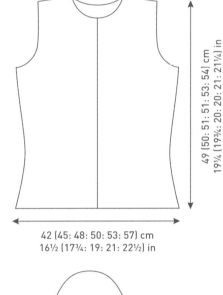

49 (50: 51: 51: 53: 54) cm
19¼ (19¾: 20: 20: 21: 21¼) in

42 (45: 48: 50: 53: 57) cm
16½ (17¾: 19: 21: 22½) in

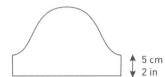

5 cm
2 in

EMBER

JACKET WITH SNUG COLLAR & EPAULETS

Recommendation
Suitable for the knitter with a little experience
Please see pages 26, 27 & 32 for photographs.

	XS	S	M	L	XL	XXL	
To fit	81	86	91	97	102	109	cm
bust	32	34	36	38	40	43	in

Rowan Big Wool

8	8	9	9	10	11	x 100gm	

Photographed in Glum

Needles
1 pair 9mm (no 00) (US 13) needles
1 pair 10mm (no 000) (US 15) needles
1 pair 12mm (US 17) needles

Buttons – 9

Tension
10 sts and 15 rows to 10 cm measured over
pattern using 10mm (US 15) needles.

Pattern note: The number of sts varies whilst
working patt. All st counts given presume there
are 8 sts between markers at all times.

BACK
Cast on 39 (41: 43: 47: 49: 53) sts using
10mm (US 15) needles.
Row 1 (WS): K5 (6: 7: 9: 10: 12), place
marker on right needle, K8, place marker
on right needle, K13, place marker on right
needle, K8, place marker on right needle,
K5 (6: 7: 9: 10: 12).
Now work in patt as folls:
Row 1 (RS): *K to marker, slip marker onto
right needle, yfwd, K8, yfwd, slip marker onto
right needle, rep from * once more, K to end.
Row 2: K2 (0: 0: 2: 0: 1), P1 (0: 1: 1: 0:
1), (K3, P1) 0 (1: 1: 1: 2: 2) times, K2, *slip
marker onto right needle, K1, P8, K1, slip
marker onto right needle*, K2, (P1, K3) twice,
P1, K2, rep from * to * once more, K2, (P1, K3)
0 (1: 1: 1: 2: 2) times, P1 (0: 1: 1: 1: 0: 1), K2 (0:
0: 2: 0: 1).
Row 3: *K to marker, slip marker onto right
needle, K1, yfwd, K8, yfwd, K1, slip marker onto
right needle, rep from * once more, K to end.
Row 4: K0 (1: 2: 0: 1: 0), P1 (1: 1: 1: 1: 0),
(K3, P1) 1 (1: 1: 2: 2: 3) times, *slip marker
onto right needle, K2, P8, K2, slip marker onto
right needle*, (P1, K3) 3 times, P1, rep from *
to * once more, (P1, K3) 1 (1: 1: 2: 2: 3) times,
P1 (1: 1: 1: 1: 0), K0 (1: 2: 0: 1: 0).
Row 5: *K to marker, slip marker onto right
needle, K2, yfwd, K8, yfwd, K2, slip marker
onto right needle, rep from * once more,
K to end.
Row 6: K2 (0: 0: 2: 0: 1), P1 (0: 1: 1: 0:
1), (K3, P1) 0 (1: 1: 1: 2: 2) times, K2, *slip
marker onto right needle, K1, P1, K1, P8, K1,
P1, K1, slip marker onto right needle*, K2,
(P1, K3) twice, P1, K2, rep from * to * once
more, K2, (P1, K3) 0 (1: 1: 1: 2: 2) times,
P1 (0: 1: 1: 1: 0: 1), K2 (0: 0: 2: 0: 1).
Row 7: *K to marker, slip marker onto right
needle, K3, K4tog tbl, K4tog, K3, slip marker
onto right needle, rep from * once more,
K to end.
Row 8: K0 (1: 2: 0: 1: 0), P1 (1: 1: 1: 1: 0),
(K3, P1) 1 (1: 1: 2: 2: 3) times, *slip marker
onto right needle, K8, slip marker onto right
needle*, (P1, K3) 3 times, P1, rep from * to *
once more, (P1, K3) 1 (1: 1: 2: 2: 3) times,
P1 (1: 1: 1: 1: 0), K0 (1: 2: 0: 1: 0).
These 8 rows form patt.

Cont in patt, shaping side seams by inc
1 st at each end of 7th and foll 14th row.
43 (45: 47: 51: 53: 57) sts.
Work 7 (7: 9: 9: 9: 9) rows, ending with a WS
row. (Back should measure 25 (25: 26: 26:
26: 26) cm.)
Shape armholes
Keeping patt correct, cast off 3 sts at beg of
next 2 rows. 37 (39: 41: 45: 47: 51) sts.
Dec 1 st at each end of next 1 (2: 2: 4: 4: 6)
rows. 35 (35: 37: 37: 39: 39) sts.
Work 25 (24: 22: 20: 20: 26) rows, ending
after patt row 8 and with a WS row.
Now working sts between markers in st st,
not patt, cont as folls:
Work 0 (0: 2: 4: 6: 0) rows, ending with
a WS row.
Shape back neck and shoulders
Next row (RS): Cast off 5 (5: 6: 5: 6: 6) sts,
patt until there are 6 sts on right needle
and turn, leaving rem sts on a holder.
Work each side of neck separately.
Work 1 row.
Cast off rem 6 sts.
With RS facing, rejoin yarn to rem sts, cast off
centre 13 (13: 13: 15: 15: 15) sts, patt to end.
Complete to match first side, reversing
shapings.

LEFT FRONT
Cast on 23 (24: 25: 27: 28: 30) sts using
10mm (US 15) needles.
Row 1 (WS): K10, place marker on right
needle, K8, place marker on right needle,
K5 (6: 7: 9: 10: 12).
Now work in patt as folls:
Row 1 (RS): K to marker, slip marker onto
right needle, yfwd, K8, yfwd, slip marker onto
right needle, K to end.
Row 2: (K3, P1) twice, K2, slip marker onto
right needle, K1, P8, K1, slip marker onto right
needle, K2, (P1, K3) 0 (1: 1: 1: 2: 2) times,
P1 (0: 1: 1: 1: 0: 1), K2 (0: 0: 2: 0: 1).
Row 3: K to marker, slip marker onto right
needle, K1, yfwd, K8, yfwd, K1, slip marker
onto right needle, K to end.
Row 4: K5, P1, K3, P1, slip marker onto right
needle, K2, P8, K2, slip marker onto right
needle, (P1, K3) 1 (1: 1: 2: 2: 3) times, P1 (1:
1: 1: 1: 0), K0 (1: 2: 0: 1: 0).

Row 5: K to marker, slip marker onto right needle, K2, yfwd, K8, yfwd, K2, slip marker onto right needle, K to end.
Row 6: (K3, P1) twice, K2, slip marker onto right needle, K1, P1, K1, P8, K1, P1, K1, slip marker onto right needle, K2, (P1, K3) 0 (1: 1: 1: 2: 2) times, P1 (0: 1: 1: 0: 1), K2 (0: 0: 2: 0: 1).
Row 7: K to marker, slip marker onto right needle, K3, K4tog tbl, K4tog, K3, slip marker onto right needle, K to end.
Row 8: K5, P1, K3, P1, slip marker onto right needle, K8, slip marker onto right needle, (P1, K3) 1 (1: 1: 2: 2: 3) times, P1 (1: 1: 1: 1: 0), K0 (1: 2: 0: 1: 0).
These 8 rows form patt.
Cont in patt, shaping side seam by inc 1 st at beg of 7th and foll 14th row.
25 (26: 27: 29: 30: 32) sts.
Work 7 (7: 9: 9: 9: 9) rows, ending with a WS row.
Shape armhole
Keeping patt correct, cast off 3 sts at beg of next row. 22 (23: 24: 26: 27: 29) sts.
Work 1 row.
Dec 1 st at armhole edge of next 1 (2: 2: 4: 4: 6) rows.
21 (21: 22: 22: 23: 23) sts.
Keeping patt correct as set by back (by working sts between markers in st st for last few rows at shoulder edge), cont as folls:
Work 17 (16: 16: 14: 16: 16) rows, ending with a WS row.
Shape neck
Next row (RS): Patt to last 6 sts and turn, leaving rem 6 sts on a holder.
15 (15: 16: 16: 17: 17) sts.
Keeping patt correct, dec 1 st at neck edge of next 2 rows, then on foll 2 (2: 2: 3: 3: 3) alt rows. 11 (11: 12: 11: 12: 12) sts.
Work 1 row, ending with a WS row.
Shape shoulder
Cast off 5 (5: 6: 5: 6: 6) sts at beg of next row.
Work 1 row.
Cast off rem 6 sts.
Mark positions for 5 buttons along left front opening edge - first to come in row 5, last to come 5 rows up from beg of neck shaping, and rem 3 buttons evenly spaced between.

RIGHT FRONT
Cast on 23 (24: 25: 27: 28: 30) sts using 10mm (US 15) needles.
Row 1 (WS): K5 (6: 7: 9: 10: 12), place marker on right needle, K8, place marker on right needle, K10.
Now work in patt as folls:

Row 1 (RS): K to marker, slip marker onto right needle, yfwd, K8, yfwd, slip marker onto right needle, K to end.
Row 2: K2 (0: 0: 2: 0: 1), P1 (0: 1: 1: 0: 1), (K3, P1) 0 (1: 1: 1: 2: 2) times, K2, slip marker onto right needle, K1, P8, K1, slip marker onto right needle, K2, (P1, K3) twice.
Row 3: K to marker, slip marker onto right needle, K1, yfwd, K8, yfwd, K1, slip marker onto right needle, K to end.
Row 4: K0 (1: 2: 0: 1: 0), P1 (1: 1: 1: 1: 0), (K3, P1) 1 (1: 1: 2: 2: 3) times, slip marker onto right needle, K2, P8, K2, slip marker onto right needle, P1, K3, P1, K5.
Row 5: K2, K2tog, yfwd (to make first buttonhole), K to marker, slip marker onto right needle, K2, yfwd, K8, yfwd, K2, slip marker onto right needle, K to end.
Row 6: K2 (0: 0: 2: 0: 1), P1 (0: 1: 1: 0: 1), (K3, P1) 0 (1: 1: 1: 2: 2) times, K2, slip marker onto right needle, K1, P1, K1, P8, K1, P1, K1, slip marker onto right needle, K2, (P1, K3) twice.
Row 7: K to marker, slip marker onto right needle, K3, K4tog tbl, K4tog, K3, slip marker onto right needle, K to end.
Row 8: K0 (1: 2: 0: 1: 0), P1 (1: 1: 1: 1: 0), (K3, P1) 1 (1: 1: 2: 2: 3) times, slip marker onto right needle, K8, slip marker onto right needle, P1, K3, P1, K5.
These 8 rows form patt and place first buttonhole.
Working a further 3 buttonholes in this way to correspond with positions marked for buttons on left front and noting that no further reference will be made to buttonholes, cont as folls:
Cont in patt, shaping side seam by inc 1 st at end of 7th and foll 14th row.
25 (26: 27: 29: 30: 32) sts.
Complete to match left front, reversing shapings and working first row of neck shaping as folls:
Shape front neck
Next row (RS): Patt 6 sts and slip these sts onto a holder, patt to end.
15 (15: 16: 16: 17: 17) sts.

SLEEVES (both alike)
Cast on 21 (23: 23: 25: 25: 27) sts using 10mm (US 15) needles.
Work in patt as folls:
Row 1 (RS): Knit.
Row 2: K2 (3: 3: 0: 0: 1), *P1, K3, rep from * to last 3 (0: 0: 1: 1: 2) sts, P1 (0: 0: 1: 1: 1), K2 (0: 0: 0: 0: 1).
Row 3: Knit.

Row 4: K0 (1: 1: 2: 2: 3), *P1, K3, rep from * to last 1 (2: 2: 3: 3: 0) sts, P1 (1: 1: 1: 1: 0), K0 (1: 1: 2: 2: 0).
These 4 rows form patt.
Cont in patt, shaping sides by inc 1 st at each end of 9th (9th: 9th: 11th: 7th: 7th) and every foll 14th (14th: 16th: 16th: 12th: 12th) row to 27 (27: 31: 33: 31: 31) sts, then on every foll 16th (16th: -: -: 14th: 14th) row until there are 29 (31: -: -: 35: 37) sts, taking inc sts into patt.
Cont straight until sleeve measures 44 (45: 46: 47: 48: 49) cm, ending with a WS row.
Shape top
Keeping patt correct, cast off 3 sts at beg of next 2 rows. 23 (25: 25: 27: 29: 31) sts.
Dec 1 st at each end of next and 3 foll 4th rows, then on every foll alt row to 11 sts, then on foll row, ending with a WS row.
Cast off rem 9 sts.

MAKING UP
Press all pieces with a warm iron over a damp cloth.
Join both shoulder seams using back stitch or mattress stitch if preferred.
Collar
With RS facing and using 10mm (US 15) needles, slip 6 sts from right front holder onto right needle, rejoin yarn and pick up and knit 10 (10: 10: 11: 11: 11) sts up right side of neck, 16 (16: 16: 18: 18: 18) sts from back, and 10 (10: 10: 11: 11: 11) sts down left side of neck, then K across 6 sts on left front holder. 48 (48: 48: 52: 52: 52) sts.
Row 1 (RS of collar, WS of body): K5, *P2, K2, rep from * to last 3 sts, K3.
Row 2: K3, *P2, K2, rep from * to last st, K1.
These 2 rows form rib.
Work in rib for a further 3 rows, ending with a **RS** row.
Row 6 (buttonhole row) (WS of collar): K2, K2tog, yfrn, rib to end.
Work in rib for a further 4 rows, ending with RS of collar facing for next row.
Row 11: K4, M1, K1, *P2, K1, M1, K1, rep from * to last 3 sts, K3. 59 (59: 59: 64: 64: 64) sts.
Row 12: K3, *P3, K2, rep from * to last st, K1.
Row 13: K6, *P2, K3, rep from * to last 3 sts, K3.
Last 2 rows form rib for rest of collar.
Work 12 rows.
Change to 12mm (US 17) needles.
Work a further 5 rows.
Cast off in rib.
Sleeve tabs (make 2)
Cast on 5 sts using 9mm (US 13) needles.
Work in g st for 32 rows.
Cast off.

Epaulettes (make 2)

Cast on 5 sts using 9mm (US 13) needles.
Work in g st for 18 rows.
Cast off.
Lay epaulette over shoulder seam so that the cast-off edge matches armhole edge and sew in place at armhole edge.
Join side seams. Join sleeve seams, enclosing cast-off end of sleeve tab in sleeve seam - position tab 5 cm up from sleeve cast-on edge. Sew sleeves into armholes, enclosing end of epaulette in seam. Sew on buttons, attach one to each sleeve tab as in photograph to secure tabs in place, and one to end of each epaulette to secure in place.

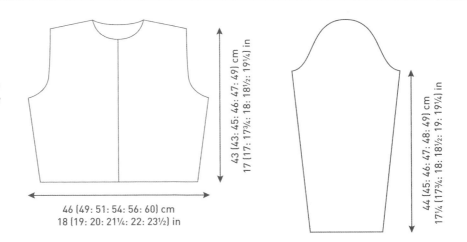

43 (43: 45: 46: 47: 49) cm
17 (17: 17¾: 18: 18½: 19¼) in

46 (49: 51: 54: 56: 60) cm
18 (19: 20: 21¼: 22: 23½) in

44 (45: 46: 47: 48: 49) cm
17¼ (17¾: 18: 18½: 19: 19¼) in

COMET

V-NECK VEST WITH CAP SLEEVES WITH OPTIONAL SNOOD

Recommendation

Suitable for the knitter with a little experience
Please see pages 28 & 29 for photographs.

	XS	S	M	L	XL	XXL	
To fit	**81**	**86**	**91**	**97**	**102**	**109**	cm
bust	32	34	36	38	40	43	in

Rowan Kidsilk Aura
Vest

| | 5 | 6 | 6 | 7 | 7 | 8 | x 25gm |

For **snood**, you will need an extra
4 x 25gm balls
Both photographed in Pumice

Needles

1 pair 3¼mm (no 10) (US 3) needles
1 pair 5½mm (no 5) (US 9) needles
Snood only: 1 pair 6mm (no 4) (US 10)
needles

Tension

Vest:
15 sts and 20 rows to 10 cm measured over
stocking stitch using 5 ½ mm (US 9) needles.
Snood:
15 sts and 18 rows to 10 cm using 6 mm (US
10) needles.

VEST
BACK

Cast on 64 (68: 72: 76: 80: 86) sts using
5½mm (US 9) needles.
Beg with a K row, now work in st st throughout
as folls:
Work 12 rows.
Next row (dec) (RS): K2, K2tog, K to last 4 sts,
K2tog tbl, K2.
Working all side seam decreases as set by last
row, dec 1 st at each end of 8th and 3 foll 8th
rows.
54 (58: 62: 66: 70: 76) sts.
Cont straight until back measures 30 (30: 31:
31: 31: 31) cm, ending with a WS row.
Next row (inc) (RS): K2, M1, K to last 2 sts,
M1, K2.**
Working all side seam increases as set by
last row, inc 1 st at each end of 12th and
foll 12th row.
60 (64: 68: 72: 76: 82) sts.
Work 7 rows, ending with a WS row. (Back
should measure 46 (46: 47: 47: 47: 47) cm.)
Shape armholes
Cast off 4 (5: 5: 6: 6: 7) sts at beg of next
2 rows.
52 (54: 58: 60: 64: 68) sts.
Next row (RS): K2, K2tog, K to last 4 sts,
K2tog tbl, K1, pick up loop lying between
needles and place this loop on right needle
(**note**: this loop does **NOT** count as a st),
sl last st purlwise.
Next row: P tog first st and the picked-up
loop, (P1, P2tog tbl) 0 (0: 0: 0: 1: 1) times,
P to last 1 (1: 1: 1: 4: 4) sts, (P2tog, P1)
0 (0: 0: 0: 1: 1) times, pick up loop lying
between needles and place this loop on
right needle (**note**: this loop does **NOT**
count as a st), sl last st knitwise.
Next row: K tog first st and the picked-up
loop, K1, K2tog, K to last 4 sts, K2tog tbl,
K1, pick up loop lying between needles
and place this loop on right needle (**note**:
this loop does **NOT** count as a st), sl last
st purlwise.
48 (50: 54: 56: 58: 62) sts.
Last 2 rows set form slip st edging.
Working all armhole decreases and
increases in same way as side seam
shaping, cont as folls:

Dec 0 (0: 1: 1: 1: 1) st at each end of 0 (0:
2nd: 2nd: 2nd: 2nd) and foll 0 (0: 0: 0: 0: 1)
alt row.
48 (50: 52: 54: 56: 58) sts.
Work 5 (7: 5: 7: 9: 9) rows, ending with
a WS row.
Inc 1 st at each end of next and foll 4th
row, then on foll 5 alt rows, then on foll
2 rows.
66 (68: 70: 72: 74: 76) sts.
Work 5 rows, ending with a WS row.
Shape shoulders and back neck
Cast off 3 sts at beg of next 2 rows, then
4 sts at beg of foll 2 rows, then 5 sts at
beg of foll 2 rows.
42 (44: 46: 48: 50: 52) sts.
Next row (RS): Cast off 5 (6: 6: 6: 7: 7) sts,
K until there are 10 (10: 11: 11: 11: 12) sts
on right needle and turn, leaving rem sts on
a holder.
Work each side of neck separately.
Cast off 4 sts at beg of next row.
Cast off rem 6 (6: 7: 7: 7: 8) sts.
With RS facing, rejoin yarn to rem sts, cast off
centre 12 (12: 12: 14: 14: 14) sts, K to end.
Complete to match first side, reversing
shapings.

FRONT

Work as given for back to **.
Working all side seam increases as set by
last row, inc 1 st at each end of 12th row.
58 (62: 66: 70: 74: 80) sts.
Work 7 rows, ending with a WS row.
Divide for neck
Next row (RS): K25 (27: 29: 31: 33: 36),
K2tog tbl, K1, pick up loop lying between
needles and place this loop on right needle
(**note**: this loop does **NOT** count as a st),
sl next st purlwise and turn, leaving rem sts
on a holder.
Work each side of neck separately.
Working slip st edging along neck edge in
same way as for back armhole and all neck
decreases as set by last row, cont as folls:
Dec 1 st at neck edge of 4th and foll 4th row
and at same time inc 1 st at side seam edge
of 4th row.
27 (29: 31: 33: 35: 38) sts.
Work 3 rows, ending with a WS row.

Shape armhole

Cast off 4 (5: 5: 6: 6: 7) sts at beg and dec 1 st at end of next row.
22 (23: 25: 26: 28: 30) sts.
Work 1 row.
Working slip st edging along armhole edge in same way as for back and all armhole decreases and increases in same way as side seam shaping, cont as folls:
Dec 1 st at armhole edge of next 1 (1: 1: 1: 3: 3) rows, then on foll 1 (1: 2: 2: 1: 2) alt rows **and at same time** dec 1 st at neck edge of 3rd and 0 (0: 0: 0: 0: 1) foll 4th row.
19 (20: 21: 22: 23: 23) sts.
Work 5 (7: 5: 7: 9: 9) rows, dec 1 st at neck edge of 4th (4th: 2nd: 2nd: 2nd: 4th) and 0 (0: 0: 1: 1: 1) foll 4th row and ending with a WS row. 18 (19: 20: 20: 21: 21) sts.
Inc 1 st at armhole edge of next and foll 4th row, then on foll 5 alt rows, then on foll 2 rows **and at same time** dec 1 st at neck edge of 3rd (next: next: 3rd: next: 3rd) and 3 (3: 3: 3: 3: 2) foll 4th rows. 23 (24: 25: 25: 26: 27) sts.
Work 5 rows, ending with a WS row.
Shape shoulder
Cast off 3 sts at beg of next row, then 4 sts at beg of foll alt row, 5 sts at beg of foll alt row, then 5 (6: 6: 6: 7: 7) sts at beg of foll alt row.
Work 1 row.
Cast off rem 6 (6: 7: 7: 7: 8) sts.
With RS facing, rejoin yarn to rem sts, K2, K2tog, K to end.
Complete to match first side, reversing shapings.

BACK NECKBAND

With RS facing and using 3¼mm (US 3) needles, pick up and knit 20 (20: 20: 22: 22: 22) sts across back neck edge.
Cast off quite loosely knitwise (on **WS**).

MAKING UP

Press all pieces with a warm iron over a damp cloth.
Join both shoulder seams using back stitch or mattress stitch if preferred. Join side seams.

SNOOD

Cast on 71 sts using 6mm (US 10) needles.
Row 1 (RS): Cast on 1 st, cast off 1 st, K to end.
Row 2: Cast on 1 st, cast off 1 st (one st on right needle), K3, *sl 1, K2tog, psso, (yfwd) twice, rep from * to last 4 sts, K4.
Row 3: Cast on 1 st, cast off 1 st (one st on right needle), K3, *(P1, K1) into double yfwd of previous row, P1, rep from * to last 4 sts, K4.

Rows 4 to 6: As rows 1 to 3.
These 6 rows form patt.
Cont in patt until snood measures approx 100 cm, ending after patt row 1 and with a **RS** row.
Cast off (on **WS**).
Join cast-on and cast-off edges to form a tube.

46 (46: 47: 47: 47: 47) cm
19 (20: 20: 21: 22: 23) in

40.5 (43: 45.5: 48: 50.5: 54.5) cm
16 (17: 18: 19: 20: 21½) in

MYSTERY

Recommendation

Suitable for the knitter with a little experience
Please see pages 19, 20 & 21 for photographs.

	XS	S	M	L	XL	XXL	
To fit	**81**	**86**	**91**	**97**	**102**	**109**	cm
bust	32	34	36	38	40	43	in

Rowan Kid Classic

| | 7 | 8 | 8 | 9 | 9 | 10 | x 50gm |

Photographed in Bittersweet

Needles

1 pair 3¾mm (no 9) (US 5) needles
1 pair 4mm (no 8) (US 6) needles
1 pair 4½mm (no 7) (US 7) needles

Buttons – 12

Tension

21 sts and 27 rows to 10 cm measured over
stocking stitch using 4½mm (US 7) needles.

BACK

Cast on 91 (97: 103: 109: 115: 123) sts using
4mm (US 6) needles.
Row 1 (RS): K0 (0: 0: 0: 0: 1), P1, *K2, P1, rep
from * to last 0 (0: 0: 0: 0: 1) st, K0 (0: 0: 0: 0: 1).
Row 2: P0 (0: 0: 0: 0: 1), K1, *P2, K1, rep from
* to last 0 (0: 0: 0: 0: 1) st, P0 (0: 0: 0: 0: 1).
These 2 rows form rib.
Work in rib for a further 10 rows, ending with
a WS row.
Change to 4½mm (US 7) needles.
Beg with a K row, now work in st st throughout
as folls:
Work 8 rows, ending with a WS row.
Next row (dec) (RS): K3, K2tog, K to last 5 sts,
K2tog tbl, K3.
Working all side seam decreases as set by last
row, dec 1 st at each end of 6th and 4 foll 6th
rows. 79 (85: 91: 97: 103: 111) sts.
Cont straight until back measures 25 (25: 26:
26: 26: 26) cm, ending with a WS row.
Next row (inc) (RS): K3, M1, K to last 3 sts,
M1, K3.
Working all side seam increases as set by last
row, inc 1 st at each end of 8th and 2 foll 8th
rows, then on foll 10th row.
89 (95: 101: 107: 113: 121) sts.
Work 9 rows, ending with a WS row. (Back
should measures 41 (41: 42: 42: 42: 42) cm).
Shape armholes
Cast off 3 (4: 4: 5: 5: 6) sts at beg of next
2 rows. 83 (87: 93: 97: 103: 109) sts.
Dec 1 st at each end of next 5 (5: 7: 7: 9: 9)
rows, then on foll 3 (4: 4: 5: 5: 6) alt rows,
then on foll 4th row.
65 (67: 69: 71: 73: 77) sts.
Cont straight until armhole measures 18 (19:
19: 20: 21: 22) cm, ending with a WS row.
Shape back neck and shoulders
Cast off 6 (6: 6: 6: 7: 7) sts at beg of next 2
rows. 53 (55: 57: 59: 59: 63) sts.
Next row (RS): Cast off 6 (6: 6: 6: 7: 7) sts, K
until there are 10 (10: 11: 11: 10: 12) sts on
right needle and turn, leaving rem sts on a holder.
Work each side of neck separately.
Cast off 4 sts at beg of next row.
Cast off rem 6 (6: 7: 7: 6: 8) sts.
With RS facing, rejoin yarn to rem sts, cast off
centre 21 (23: 23: 25: 25: 25) sts, K to end.
Complete to match first side, reversing shapings.

POCKET LININGS (make 2)

Cast on 21 (21: 23: 23: 25: 25) sts using
4½mm (US 7) needles.
Beg with a K row, work in st st for 24 rows,
ending with a WS row.
Break yarn and leave sts on a holder.

LEFT FRONT

Cast on 52 (55: 58: 61: 64: 68) sts using
4mm (US 6) needles.
Row 1 (RS): K0 (0: 0: 0: 0: 1), P1, *K2, P1, rep
from * to last 9 sts, K2, (P1, K1) 3 times, P1.
Row 2: P1, (K1, P1) 3 times, *P2, K1, rep from
* to last 0 (0: 0: 0: 0: 1) st, P0 (0: 0: 0: 0: 1).
Row 3: K0 (0: 0: 0: 0: 1), P1, *K2, P1, rep
from * to last 9 sts, K2, (K1, P1) 3 times, K1.
Row 4: K1, (P1, K1) 3 times, *P2, K1, rep
from * to last 0 (0: 0: 0: 0: 1) st, P0 (0: 0: 0: 0: 1).
These 4 rows set the sts - front opening edge
7 sts in double moss st with all other sts in rib.
Cont as set for a further 8 rows, ending with
a WS row.
Change to 4½mm (US 7) needles.
Row 13 (RS): K to last 7 sts, patt 7 sts.
Row 14: Patt 7 sts, P to end.
These 2 rows set the sts for rest of left front -
front opening edge 7 sts still in double moss
st with all other sts now in st st.
Keeping sts correct as now set, cont as folls:
Work 6 rows, ending with a WS row.
Working all side seam shaping as set by
back, dec 1 st at beg of next and 2 foll
6th rows. 49 (52: 55: 58: 61: 65) sts.
Work 3 rows, ending with a WS row.
Place pocket
Next row (RS): K9 (11: 11: 12: 12: 13), slip
next 21 (21: 23: 23: 25: 25) sts onto a holder
and, in their place, K across 21 (21: 23: 23:
25: 25) sts of first pocket lining, patt to end.
Dec 1 st at beg of 2nd and 2 foll 6th rows.
46 (49: 52: 55: 58: 62) sts.
Cont straight until left front measures 25 (25:
26: 26: 26: 26) cm, ending with a WS row.
Working all side seam increases as set by
back, inc 1 st at beg of next row.
47 (50: 53: 56: 59: 63) sts.
Work 1 row, ending with a WS row.
Shape front slope
Next row (RS): K to last 9 sts, K2tog tbl,
patt 7 sts.

Working all front slope decreases as set by last row, cont as folls:

Dec 1 st at front slope edge on 6th (6th: 6th: 4th: 4th: 6th) and 0 (0: 0: 1: 0: 0) foll 4th rows, then on 5 (5: 5: 5: 6: 5) foll 6th rows **and at same time** inc 1 st at side seam edge of 6th and 2 foll 6th rows, then on foll 8th row. 44 (47: 50: 52: 55: 60) sts.

Work 5 (5: 5: 3: 1: 5) rows, ending with a WS row.

Shape armhole

Keeping sts correct, cast off 3 (4: 4: 5: 5: 6) sts at beg and dec 1 (1: 1: 0: 0: 1) st at end of next row. 40 (42: 45: 47: 50: 53) sts.

Work 1 row.

Dec 1 st at armhole edge of next 5 (5: 7: 7: 9: 9) rows, then on foll 3 (4: 4: 5: 5: 6) alt rows, then on foll 4th row **and at same time** dec 1 st at front slope edge on 5th (5th: 5th: next: 3rd: 5th) and 1 (2: 2: 3: 3: 3) foll 6th rows. 29 (29: 30: 30: 31: 33) sts.

Dec 1 st at front slope edge **only** on 2nd (6th: 4th: 4th: 4th: 4th) and 2 (3: 3: 3: 3: 2) foll 6th rows, then on 1 (0: 0: 0: 0: 1) foll 8th row. 25 (25: 26: 26: 27: 29) sts.

Cont straight until left front matches back to beg of shoulder shaping, ending with a WS row.

Shape shoulder

Cast off 6 (6: 6: 6: 7: 7) sts at beg of next and foll alt row, then 6 (6: 7: 7: 6: 8) sts at beg of foll alt row.

Cont in double moss st on rem 7 sts only (for back neck border extension) for a further 7 (7: 7: 7.5: 7.5: 7.5) cm, ending with a WS row. Cast off.

Mark positions for 6 buttons along left front opening edge - first button to come in row 5, 2nd button to come in row 13, top button to come just below start of front slope shaping, and rem 3 buttons evenly spaced between top button and 2nd button.

RIGHT FRONT

Cast on 52 (55: 58: 61: 64: 68) sts using 4mm (US 6) needles.

Row 1 (RS): P1, (K1, P1) 3 times, *K2, P1, rep from * to last 0 (0: 0: 0: 0: 1) st, K0 (0: 0: 0: 0: 1).

Row 2: P0 (0: 0: 0: 0: 1), K1, *P2, K1, rep from * to last 9 sts, P2, (P1, K1) 3 times, P1.

Row 3: K1, (P1, K1) 3 times, *K2, P1, rep from * to last 0 (0: 0: 0: 0: 1) st, K0 (0: 0: 0: 0: 1).

Row 4: P0 (0: 0: 0: 0: 1), K1, *P2, K1, rep from * to last 9 sts, P2, (K1, P1) 3 times, K1.

These 4 rows set the sts - front opening edge 7 sts in double moss st with all other sts in rib.

Row 5 (buttonhole row) (RS): Patt 2 sts, work 2 tog, yrn (to make a buttonhole), patt to end.

Working a further 5 buttonholes in this way to correspond with positions marked for buttons on left front and noting that no further reference will be made to buttonholes (except for buttonhole in row 13), cont as folls:

Work 7 rows, ending with a WS row.

Change to 4½mm (US 7) needles.

Row 13 (RS): Patt 2 sts, work 2 tog, yrn (to make 2nd buttonhole), patt 3 sts, K to end.

Row 14: P to last 7 sts, patt 7 sts.

These 2 rows set the sts for rest of right front - front opening edge 7 sts still in double moss st with all other sts now in st st.

Keeping sts correct as now set, cont as folls:

Work 6 rows, ending with a WS row.

Working all side seam shaping as set by back, dec 1 st at end of next and 2 foll 6th rows. 49 (52: 55: 58: 61: 65) sts.

Work 3 rows, ending with a WS row.

Place pocket

Next row (RS): Patt 19 (20: 21: 23: 24: 27) sts, slip next 21 (21: 23: 23: 25: 25) sts onto a holder and, in their place, K across 21 (21: 23: 23: 25: 25) sts of second pocket lining, K to end.

Dec 1 st at end of 2nd and 2 foll 6th rows. 46 (49: 52: 55: 58: 62) sts.

Cont straight until right front measures 25 (25: 26: 26: 26: 26) cm, ending with a WS row.

Working all side seam increases as set by back, inc 1 st at end of next row. 47 (50: 53: 56: 59: 63) sts.

Work 1 row, ending with a WS row.

Shape front slope

Next row (RS): Patt 7 sts, K2tog, K to end.

Working all front slope decreases as set by last row, complete to match left front, reversing shapings.

SLEEVES (both alike)

Cast on 39 (41: 43: 45: 47: 49) sts using 4mm (US 6) needles.

Row 1 (RS): K1 (2: 0: 1: 2: 0), *P1, K2, rep from * to last 2 (0: 1: 2: 0: 1) sts, P1 (0: 1: 1: 0: 1), K1 (0: 0: 1: 0: 0).

Row 2: P1 (2: 0: 1: 2: 0), *K1, P2, rep from * to last 2 (0: 1: 2: 0: 1) sts, K1 (0: 1: 1: 0: 1), P1 (0: 0: 1: 0: 0).

These 2 rows form rib.

Work in rib for a further 12 rows, ending with a WS row.

Change to 4½mm (US 7) needles.

Working all sleeve increases in same way as side seam increases and beg with a K row, now work in st st, shaping sides by inc 1 st at each end of 3rd and every foll 8th row to 59 (59: 57: 57: 57: 55) sts, then on every

foll 10th row until there are 63 (65: 67: 69: 71: 73) sts.

Cont straight until sleeve measures 45 (46: 47: 48: 49: 50) cm, ending with a WS row.

Shape top

Cast off 3 (4: 4: 5: 5: 6) sts at beg of next 2 rows. 57 (57: 59: 59: 61: 61) sts.

Dec 1 st at each end of next 3 rows, then on foll alt row, then on 4 (5: 4: 5: 5: 6) foll 4th rows. 41 (39: 43: 41: 43: 41) sts.

Work 1 row, ending with a WS row.

Dec 1 st at each end of next and foll 3 (2: 4: 3: 4: 3) alt rows, then on foll 5 rows, ending with a WS row. Cast off rem 23 sts.

MAKING UP

Press all pieces with a warm iron over a damp cloth.

Join both shoulder seams using back stitch or mattress stitch if preferred. Join cast-off ends of back neck border extensions, then sew one edge to back neck.

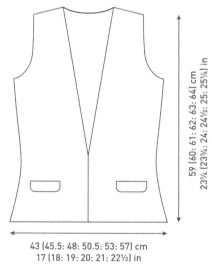

43 (45.5: 48: 50.5: 53: 57) cm
17 (18: 19: 20: 21: 22½) in

59 (60: 61: 62: 63: 64) cm
23¼ (23¾: 24: 24½: 25: 25¼) in

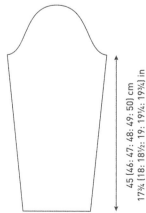

45 (46: 47: 48: 49: 50) cm
17¾ (18: 18½: 19: 19¼: 19¾) in

Continued on next page...

HEATH

Rowan Drift or Big Wool
    4   x 100gm
Photographed in Driftwood

Rowan Kidsilk Haze
    4   x 25gm
Photographed in Pearl

Needles
Drift/Big Wool scarf: 1 pair 12mm (US 17) needles

Kidsilk Haze scarf: 1 pair 6mm (no 4) (US 10) needles

Tension
Drift/Big Wool scarf: 9 sts and 12 rows to 10 cm measured over pattern using 12mm (US 17) needles.

Kidsilk Haze scarf: 15 sts and 18 rows to 10 cm measured over pattern using 6mm (US 10) needles.

Finished size
Drift/Big Wool scarf: Completed scarf measures approx 240 cm (94½ ins) long and is 24 cm (9½ ins) wide.
Kidsilk Haze scarf: Completed scarf measures approx 200 cm (78½ ins) long and is 31 cm (12 ins) wide.

Recommendation
Suitable for the knitter with a little experience
Please see pages 14, 15 & 19 for photographs.

Kidsilk Haze scarf pattern note: Use Kidsilk Haze DOUBLE throughout.

Pattern note: Instructions are given for both scarves. First set of figures relate to Drift/Big Wool scarf, with figures for Kidsilk Haze scarf given in bold in square brackets. Where one set of figures is given, this relates to both scarves.

SCARF
Cast on 22 [**47**] sts using 12mm (US 17) [**6mm (US 10)**] needles.
Row 1 (RS): Cast on 1 st, cast off 1 st, K to end.
Row 2: Cast on 1 st, cast off 1 st (one st on right needle), K1 [**3**], *sl 1, K2tog, psso, (yfwd) twice, rep from * to last 2 [**4**] sts, K2 [**4**].
Row 3: Cast on 1 st, cast off 1 st (one st on right needle), K1 [**3**], *(K1, P1) into double yfwd of previous row, P1, rep from * to last 2 [**4**] sts, K2 [**4**].
Rows 4 to 6: As rows 1 to 3.
These 6 rows form patt.
Cont in patt until scarf measures approx 240 [**200**] cm, ending after patt row 1 and with a **RS** row.
(**Note:** If preferred, cont until almost all yarn has been used up, ending after patt row 1 or 4, and leaving sufficient yarn to cast off.)
Cast off (on **WS**).

MYSTERY – *Continued from previous page.*

Pocket flaps (both alike)
Slip 21 (21: 23: 23: 25: 25) sts from pocket holder onto 3¾mm (US 5) needles and rejoin yarn with **WS** facing.
Row 1 (RS of flap, WS of front): (K1, P1) twice, M1, K4 (4: 5: 5: 6: 6), M1, K5, M1, K4 (4: 5: 5: 6: 6), M1, (P1, K1) twice.
25 (25: 27: 27: 29: 29) sts.
Row 2: (K1, P1) twice, P to last 4 sts, (P1, K1) twice.
Row 3: (K1, P1) twice, K to last 4 sts, (P1, K1) twice.

Rows 4 to 13: As rows 2 and 3, 5 times.
Row 14: K1, *P1, K1, rep from * to end.
Rows 15 to 17: As row 14.
Cast off in moss st.
Sew pocket linings in place on inside. Fold last 13 rows of pocket flap onto RS and secure in place by attaching 2 buttons as in photograph.
Epaulettes (make 2)
Cast on 7 sts using 3¾mm (US 5) needles.
Row 1 (RS): K1, (P1, K1) 3 times.
Row 2: As row 1.
These 2 rows form moss st.

Cont in moss st for a further 24 rows, ending with a WS row.
Cast off in moss st.
Lay epaulette over shoulder seam so that cast-off edge matches armhole edge and sew in place at armhole edge.
Join side seams. Join sleeve seams. Sew sleeves into armholes, enclosing end of epaulette in seam.
Attach a button to end of each epaulette to secure in place, attaching button through both layers. Sew on buttons.

WINTER

CAPE STYLE COAT WITH POCKETS & CURVED HEMLINE

Recommendation

Suitable for the knitter with a little experience
Please see pages 40, 41 & 42 for photographs.

	XS	S	M	L	XL	XXL	
To fit	81	86	91	97	102	109	cm
bust	32	34	36	38	40	43	in

Rowan Felted Tweed Chunky

	20	21	22	24	25	27	x 50gm

Photographed in Clay

Needles

1 pair 6½mm (no 3) (US 10½) needles
1 pair 7mm (no 2) (US 10½/11) needles

Buttons – 5

Tension

11½ sts and 20 rows to 10 cm measured over
moss stitch using 7mm (US 10½/11) needles.

BACK

Cast on 55 (57: 59: 63: 65: 71) sts using
7mm (US 10½/11) needles.
Row 1 (RS): K1, *P1, K1, rep from * to
last 18 sts, wrap next st (by slipping next
st on left needle onto right needle, taking
yarn to opposite side of work between
needles and then slipping same st back
onto left needle - when working back
across wrapped sts work the wrapped
st and the wrapping loop tog as one st)
and turn.
Row 2: K1, *P1, K1, rep from * to last 18 sts,
wrap next st and turn.
These 2 rows set position of moss st.
Keeping moss st correct as now set, cont as
folls:
Rows 3 and 4: Moss st to last 15 sts, wrap
next st and turn.
Rows 5 and 6: Moss st to last 12 sts, wrap
next st and turn.
Rows 7 and 8: Moss st to last 10 sts, wrap
next st and turn.
Rows 9 and 10: Moss st to last 8 sts, wrap
next st and turn.
Rows 11 and 12: Moss st to last 6 sts, wrap
next st and turn.
Rows 13 and 14: Moss st to last 4 sts, wrap
next st and turn.
Rows 15 and 16: Moss st to last 2 sts, wrap
next st and turn.
Rows 17 and 18: Moss st to end.
Row 19 (RS): Inc in first st, moss st to last
-2 sts, inc in next st, moss st 1 st.
57 (59: 61: 65: 67: 73) sts.
Working all increases as set by last row,
inc 1 st at each end of 2nd and foll 3 alt
rows, then on foll 4th row, taking inc sts
into moss st.
67 (69: 71: 75: 77: 83) sts.
Place markers at both ends of last row
to denote base of side seams.
Cont in moss st, shaping side seams
by inc 1 st at each end of 20th and foll
20th row.
71 (73: 75: 79: 81: 87) sts.
Work 21 (21: 23: 23: 23: 23) rows, ending
with a WS row.
(Back should measure 46 (46: 47: 47: 47: 47)
cm at centre of work.)

Shape raglan armholes

Cast off 4 sts at beg of next 2 rows.
63 (65: 67: 71: 73: 79) sts.
Work 2 rows.
Dec 1 st at each end of next and 4 (5: 4: 4:
4: 2) foll 4th rows, then on every foll alt row
until 17 (19: 19: 21: 21: 21) sts rem.
Work 1 row, ending with a WS row.
Cast off.

LEFT FRONT

Cast on 33 (34: 35: 37: 38: 41) sts using
7mm (US 10½/11) needles.
Row 1 (RS): *K1, P1, rep from * to last 9 (8:
9: 9: 8: 9) sts, P1 (0: 1: 1: 0: 1), K8.
Row 2: K9 (10: 9: 9: 10: 9), *P1, K1, rep from
* to last 18 sts, wrap next st and turn.
These 2 rows set the sts - front opening edge
8 sts in g st with one st in rev st st next to
these sts, and rem sts in moss st.
Keeping sts correct as now set, cont as folls:
Row 3: Patt to end.
Row 4: Moss st to last 15 sts, wrap next st
and turn.
Row 5: Patt to end.
Row 6: Moss st to last 12 sts, wrap next st
and turn.
Row 7: Patt to end.
Row 8: Moss st to last 10 sts, wrap next st
and turn.
Row 9: Patt to end.
Row 10: Moss st to last 8 sts, wrap next st
and turn.
Row 11: Patt to end.
Row 12: Moss st to last 6 sts, wrap next st
and turn.
Row 13: Patt to end.
Row 14: Moss st to last 4 sts, wrap next st
and turn.
Row 15: Patt to end.
Rows 16: Moss st to last 2 sts, wrap next st
and turn.
Rows 17 and 18: Patt to end.
Row 19 (RS): Inc in first st, patt to end.
34 (35: 36: 38: 39: 42) sts.
Working all increases as set by last row,
inc 1 st at beg of 2nd and foll 3 alt rows,
then on foll 4th row, taking inc sts into
moss st.
39 (40: 41: 43: 44: 47) sts.

Place marker at beg of last row to denote base of side seam.
Work 7 rows, ending with a WS row.

Place pocket
Next row (RS): Patt 7 (8: 9: 11: 12: 15) sts and slip these sts onto a holder, K5, patt to end. 32 sts.
Next row: Patt to last 5 sts, K5.
Next row: K5, patt to end.
Rep last 2 rows 13 times more, then first of these rows again, ending with a WS row. Break yarn and leave these 32 sts on a 2nd holder.
Return to sts left on first holder and rejoin yarn with **WS** facing, cast on 23 sts, then patt to end. 30 (31: 32: 34: 35: 38) sts.
Working all sts in moss st, work 28 rows, inc 1 st at beg of 11th of these rows and ending with a WS row.
31 (32: 33: 35: 36: 39) sts.

Join sections
Next row (RS): Moss st 8 (9: 10: 12: 13: 16) sts, holding WS of pocket front against RS of pocket back, K tog first st of pocket front with next st of pocket back, (K tog next st of pocket front with next st of pocket back) 4 times, (moss st next st of pocket front with next st of pocket back) 18 times, patt to end.
40 (41: 42: 44: 45: 48) sts.
Next row: Patt 9 sts, moss st to end.
Keeping sts correct as now set, inc 1 st at beg of next row. 41 (42: 43: 45: 46: 49) sts.
Work 21 (21: 23: 23: 23: 23) rows, ending with a WS row.

Shape raglan armhole
Cast off 4 sts at beg of next row.
37 (38: 39: 41: 42: 45) sts.
Work 3 rows.
Dec 1 st at raglan armhole edge of next and 4 (5: 4: 4: 4: 2) foll 4th rows, then on every foll alt row until 21 (22: 22: 24: 24: 24) sts rem.
Work 1 row, ending with a WS row.

Shape front neck
Next row (RS): Work 2 tog, patt 8 (8: 8: 10: 10: 10) sts and turn, leaving rem 11 (12: 12: 12: 12: 12) sts on a holder.
Dec 1 st at neck edge of next 4 rows, then on foll 1 (1: 1: 2: 2: 2) alt rows **and at same time** dec 1 st at raglan armhole edge of 2nd and foll 2 (2: 2: 3: 3: 3) alt rows. 1 st.
Work 1 row, ending with a WS row.
Fasten off.
Mark positions for 5 buttons along left front opening edge - first button to come in row 37, top button to come just above neck shaping, and rem 3 buttons evenly spaced between.

RIGHT FRONT
Cast on 33 (34: 35: 37: 38: 41) sts using 7mm (US 10½/11) needles.
Row 1 (RS): K8, P1 (0: 1: 1: 0: 0), *P1, K1, rep from * to last 18 sts, wrap next st and turn.
Row 2: *K1, P1, rep from * to last 9 (10: 9: 9: 10: 9) sts, K9 (10: 9: 9: 10: 9).
These 2 rows set the sts - front opening edge 8 sts in g st with one st in rev st st next to these sts, and rem sts in moss st.
Keeping sts correct as now set, cont as folls:
Row 3: Patt to last 15 sts, wrap next st and turn.
Row 4: Patt to end.
Row 5: Patt to last 12 sts, wrap next st and turn.
Row 6: Patt to end.
Row 7: Patt to last 10 sts, wrap next st and turn.
Row 8: Patt to end.
Row 9: Patt to last 8 sts, wrap next st and turn.
Row 10: Patt to end.
Row 11: Patt to last 6 sts, wrap next st and turn.
Row 12: Patt to end.
Row 13: Patt to last 4 sts, wrap next st and turn.
Row 14: Patt to end.
Rows 15: Patt to last 2 sts, wrap next st and turn.
Rows 16 and 18: Patt to end.
Row 19 (RS): Patt to last 2 sts, inc in next st, moss st 1 st.
34 (35: 36: 38: 39: 42) sts.
Working all increases as set by last row, inc 1 st at end of 2nd and foll 3 alt rows, then on foll 4th row, taking inc sts into moss st.
39 (40: 41: 43: 44: 47) sts.
Place marker at end of last row to denote base of side seam.
Work 5 rows, ending with a WS row.
Next row (buttonhole row) (RS): K3, K2tog tbl, yfwd (to make a buttonhole), patt to end.
Working a further 3 buttonholes in this way to correspond with positions marked for buttons on left front and noting that no further reference will be made to buttonholes, cont as folls:
Work 1 row, ending with a WS row.

Place pocket
Next row (RS): Patt 27 sts, K5 and turn, leaving rem 7 (8: 9: 11: 12: 15) sts on a holder.
32 sts.
Next row: K5, patt to end.

Next row: Patt to last 5 sts, K5.
Rep last 2 rows 13 times more, then first of these rows again, ending with a WS row.
Leave these 32 sts on a 2nd holder - do **NOT** break yarn but set this ball of yarn aside.
Return to sts left on first holder and rejoin new ball of yarn with RS facing, cast on 23 sts, then moss st to end. 30 (31: 32: 34: 35: 38) sts.
Working all sts in moss st, work 29 rows, inc 1 st at end of 12th of these rows and ending with a WS row. 31 (32: 33: 35: 36: 39) sts.
Break yarn.

Join sections
Next row (RS): Using ball of yarn set aside with sts on 2nd holder, patt 9 sts, holding WS of pocket front against RS of pocket back, moss st tog next st of pocket front with first st of pocket back, (moss st next st of pocket front with next st of pocket back) 17 times, (K tog next st of pocket front with next st of pocket back) 5 times, moss st to end.
40 (41: 42: 44: 45: 48) sts.
Next row: Moss st to last 9 sts, patt 9 sts.
Keeping sts correct as now set, inc 1 st at end of next row. 41 (42: 43: 45: 46: 49) sts.
Complete to match left front, reversing shapings and working first row of neck shaping as folls:

Shape front neck
Next row (RS): Patt 11 (12: 12: 12: 12: 12) sts and slip these sts onto a holder, patt to last 2 sts, work 2 tog. 9 (9: 9: 11: 11: 11) sts.

SLEEVES (both alike)
Cast on 53 (55: 55: 57: 59: 61) sts using 7mm (US 10½/11) needles.
Row 1 (RS): K1, *P1, K1, rep from * to last 2 2 sts, wrap next st and turn.
Row 2: K1, *P1, K1, rep from * to last 22 sts, wrap next st and turn.
These 2 rows set position of moss st.
Keeping moss st correct as now set, cont as folls:
Rows 3 and 4: Moss st to last 19 sts, wrap next st and turn.
Rows 5 and 6: Moss st to last 16 sts, wrap next st and turn.
Rows 7 and 8: Moss st to last 14 sts, wrap next st and turn.
Rows 9 and 10: Moss st to last 12 sts, wrap next st and turn.
Rows 11 and 12: Moss st to last 10 sts, wrap next st and turn.
Rows 13 and 14: Moss st to last 6 sts, wrap next st and turn.
Rows 15 and 16: Moss st to last 4 sts, wrap next st and turn.

Rows 17 and 18: Moss st to last 2 sts, wrap next st and turn.
Rows 19 and 20: Moss st to end.
Work 8 (10: 10: 12: 14: 14) rows, ending with a WS row.
(Sleeve should measure 14 (15: 15: 16: 17: 17) cm at centre of work.)

Shape raglan
Cast off 4 sts at beg of next 2 rows.
45 (47: 47: 49: 51: 53) sts.
Work 2 rows.
Dec 1 st at each end of next and 11 foll 4th rows, then on every foll alt row until 19 sts rem.
Work 1 row, ending with a WS row.

Left sleeve only
Dec 1 st at each end of next row, then cast off 3 sts at beg of foll row. 14 sts.
Dec 1 st at beg of next row, then cast off 4 sts at beg of foll row. 9 sts.
Rep last 2 rows once more.

Right sleeve only
Cast off 4 sts at beg and dec 1 st at end of next row. 14 sts.
Work 1 row.
Rep last 2 rows twice more.

Both sleeves
Cast off rem 4 sts.

MAKING UP
Press all pieces with a warm iron over a damp cloth.
Join all raglan seams using back stitch or mattress stitch if preferred.

Neckband
With RS facing and using 6½mm (US 10½) needles, slip 11 (12: 12: 12: 12: 12) sts from right front holder onto right needle, rejoin yarn and pick up and knit 7 (7: 7: 9: 9: 9) sts up right side of neck, 13 sts from top of right sleeve, 15 (17: 17: 19: 19: 19) sts from back, 13 sts from top of left sleeve, and 7 (7: 7: 9: 9: 9) sts down left side of neck, then patt across 11 (12: 12: 12: 12: 12) sts on left front holder.
77 (81: 81: 87: 87: 87) sts.
Row 1 (WS): Knit.
Row 2: K3, K2tog tbl, yfwd, K3, P1, K to last 9 sts, P1, K8.
Row 3: Knit.
Row 4: K8, P1, K to last 9 sts, P1, K8.
Rep last 2 rows twice more, ending with **WS** facing for next row.
Cast off knitwise (on **WS**).
Join side seams above markers and sleeve seams. Sew pocket backs in place on inside. Sew on buttons.

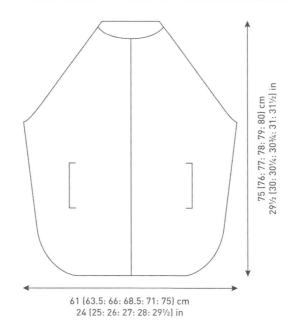

75 (76: 77: 78: 79: 80) cm
29½ (30: 30¼: 30¾: 31: 31½) in

61 (63.5: 66: 68.5: 71: 75) cm
24 (25: 26: 27: 28: 29½) in

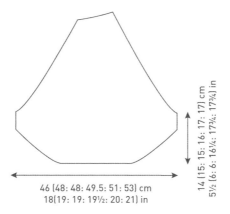

14 (15: 15: 16: 17: 17) cm
5½ (6: 6: 16¼: 17¾: 17¾) in

46 (48: 48: 49.5: 51: 53) cm
18 (19: 19: 19½: 20: 21) in

FOREST
TEXTURED DOUBLE BREASTED COAT WITH EPAULETS

Recommendation
Suitable for the knitter with a little experience
Please see page 22 for photograph.

	XS	S	M	L	XL	XXL	
To fit	81	86	91	97	102	109	cm
bust	32	34	36	38	40	43	in

Rowan Big Wool
    11   12   13   14   15   16 x 100gm
Photographed in Concrete

Needles
1 pair 9mm (no 00) (US 13) needles
1 pair 10mm (no 000) (US 15) needles

Buttons – 14 Large
          2 Small

Tension
10 sts and 15 rows to 10 cm measured over
pattern using 10mm (US 15) needles.

Pattern note: The number of sts varies whilst
working patt. All st counts given presume there
are 8 sts between markers at all times.

BACK
Cast on 49 (51: 53: 57: 59: 63) sts using
10mm (US 15) needles.
Row 1 (WS): K10 (11: 12: 14: 15: 17), place
marker on right needle, K8, place marker
on right needle, K13, place marker on right
needle, K8, place marker on right needle,
K10 (11: 12: 14: 15: 17).
Now work in patt as folls:
Row 1 (RS): *K to marker, slip marker onto
right needle, yfwd, K8, yfwd, slip marker onto
right needle, rep from * once more, K to end.
Row 2: K0 (0: 1: 0: 0: 2), P0 (1: 1: 0: 1:
1), (K3, P1) 2 (2: 2: 3: 3: 3) times, K2, *slip
marker onto right needle, K1, P8, K1, slip
marker onto right needle*, K2, (P1, K3) twice,
P1, K2, rep from * to * once more, K2, (P1, K3)
2 (2: 2: 3: 3: 3) times, P0 (1: 1: 0: 1: 1), K0 (0:
1: 0: 0: 2).
Row 3: *K to marker, slip marker onto right
needle, K1, yfwd, K8, yfwd, K1, slip marker
onto right needle, rep from * once more, K to
end.
Row 4: K1 (2: 0: 1: 2: 0), P1 (1: 0: 1: 1: 1),
(K3, P1) 2 (2: 3: 3: 3: 4) times, *slip marker
onto right needle, K2, P8, K2, slip marker onto
right needle*, (P1, K3) 3 times, P1, rep from *
to * once more, (P1, K3) 2 (2: 3: 3: 3: 4) times,
P1 (1: 0: 1: 1: 1), K1 (2: 0: 1: 2: 0).
Row 5: *K to marker, slip marker onto right
needle, K2, yfwd, K8, yfwd, K2, slip marker onto
right needle, rep from * once more, K to end.
Row 6: K0 (0: 1: 0: 0: 2), P0 (1: 1: 0: 1:
1), (K3, P1) 2 (2: 2: 3: 3: 3) times, K2, *slip
marker onto right needle, K1, P1, K1, P8, K1,
P1, K1, slip marker onto right needle*, K2, (P1,
K3) twice, P1, K2, rep from * to * once more,
K2, (P1, K3) 2 (2: 2: 3: 3: 3) times, P0 (1: 1: 0:
1: 1), K0 (0: 1: 0: 0: 2).
Row 7: *K to marker, slip marker onto right
needle, K3, K4tog tbl, K4tog, K3, slip marker
onto right needle, rep from * once more, K to
end.
Row 8: K1 (2: 0: 1: 2: 0), P1 (1: 0: 1: 1: 1),
(K3, P1) 2 (2: 3: 3: 3: 4) times, *slip marker
onto right needle, K8, slip marker onto right
needle*, (P1, K3) 3 times, P1, rep from * to *
once more, (P1, K3) 2 (2: 3: 3: 3: 4) times, P1
(1: 0: 1: 1: 1), 1 (2: 0: 1: 2: 0).
These 8 rows form patt.

Cont in patt, shaping side seams by dec
1 st at each end of 13th and 4 foll 8th rows.
39 (41: 43: 47: 49: 53) sts.
Work 15 rows, ending with a WS row.
Inc 1 st at each end of next and foll 8th row,
taking inc sts into patt.
43 (45: 47: 51: 53: 57) sts.
Work 7 (7: 9: 9: 9: 9) rows, ending with a WS
row. (Back should measure 57 (57: 58: 58:
58: 58) cm.)
Shape armholes
Keeping patt correct, cast off 3 sts at beg of
next 2 rows. 37 (39: 41: 45: 47: 51) sts.
Dec 1 st at each end of next 1 (1: 1: 3: 3: 5)
rows, then on foll 1 (2: 2: 2: 2: 2) alt rows.
33 (33: 35: 35: 37: 37) sts.
Work 23 (21: 19: 17: 17: 23) rows, ending
after patt row 8 and with a WS row.
Now working sts between markers in st st,
not patt, cont as folls:
Work 0 (2: 4: 6: 6: 0) rows, ending with a WS row.
Shape back neck and shoulders
Next row (RS): Cast off 5 sts, patt until there
are 5 (5: 6: 5: 6: 6) sts on right needle and
turn, leaving rem sts on a holder.
Work each side of neck separately.
Work 1 row.
Cast off rem 5 (5: 6: 5: 6: 6) sts.
With RS facing, rejoin yarn to rem sts, cast off
centre 13 (13: 13: 15: 15: 15) sts, patt to end.
Complete to match first side, reversing
shapings.

LEFT FRONT
Cast on 36 (37: 38: 40: 41: 43) sts using
10mm (US 15) needles.
Row 1 (WS): K18, place marker on right
needle, K8, place marker on right needle,
K10 (11: 12: 14: 15: 17).
Now work in patt as folls:
Row 1 (RS): K to marker, slip marker onto
right needle, yfwd, K8, yfwd, slip marker onto
right needle, K to end.
Row 2: (K3, P1) 4 times, K2, slip marker onto
right needle, K1, P8, K1, slip marker onto right
needle, K2, (P1, K3) 2 (2: 2: 3: 3: 3) times,
P0 (1: 1: 0: 1: 1), K0 (0: 1: 0: 0: 2).
Row 3: K to marker, slip marker onto right
needle, K1, yfwd, K8, yfwd, K1, slip marker
onto right needle, K to end.

Row 4: K5, P1, (K3, P1) 3 times, slip marker onto right needle, K2, P8, K2, slip marker onto right needle, (P1, K3) 2 (2: 3: 3: 3: 4) times, P1 (1: 0: 1: 1: 1), K1 (2: 0: 1: 2: 0).
Row 5: K to marker, slip marker onto right needle, K2, yfwd, K8, yfwd, K2, slip marker onto right needle, K to end.
Row 6: (K3, P1) 4 times, K2, slip marker onto right needle, K1, P1, K1, P8, K1, P1, K1, slip marker onto right needle, K2, (P1, K3) 2 (2: 2: 3: 3: 3) times, P0 (1: 1: 0: 1: 1), K0 (0: 1: 0: 0: 2).
Row 7: K to marker, slip marker onto right needle, K3, K4tog tbl, K4tog, K3, slip marker onto right needle, K to end.
Row 8: K5, P1, (K3, P1) 3 times, slip marker onto right needle, K8, slip marker onto right needle, (P1, K3) 2 (2: 3: 3: 3: 4) times, P1 (1: 0: 1: 1: 1), 1 (2: 0: 1: 2: 0).
These 8 rows form patt.
Cont in patt, shaping side seam by dec 1 st at beg of 13th and 4 foll 8th rows.
31 (32: 33: 35: 36: 38) sts.
Work 15 rows, ending with a WS row.
Inc 1 st at beg of next and foll 8th row, taking inc sts into patt. 33 (34: 35: 37: 38: 40) sts.
Work 7 (7: 9: 9: 9: 9) rows, ending with a WS row.

Shape armhole
Keeping patt correct, cast off 3 sts at beg of next row. 30 (31: 32: 34: 35: 37) sts.
Work 1 row.
Dec 1 st at armhole edge of next 1 (1: 1: 3: 3: 5) rows, then on foll 1 (2: 2: 2: 2: 2) alt rows.
28 (28: 29: 29: 30: 30) sts.
Keeping patt correct as set by back (by working sts between markers in st st for last few rows at shoulder edge), cont as folls:
Work 15 (15: 15: 13: 13: 13) rows, ending with a WS row.

Shape front neck
Next row (RS): Patt 15 (15: 16: 16: 17: 17) sts and turn, leaving rem 13 sts on a holder.
Keeping patt correct, dec 1 st at neck edge of next 4 rows, then on foll 1 (1: 1: 2: 2: 2) alt rows.
10 (10: 11: 10: 11: 11) sts.
Work 1 row, ending with a WS row.

Shape shoulder
Cast off 5 sts at beg of next row.
Work 1 row.
Cast off rem 5 (5: 6: 5: 6: 6) sts.
Mark positions for 5 pairs of buttons along left front opening edge - first pair to come in row 37, last pair to come 4 cm down from neck shaping, and rem 3 pairs of buttons evenly spaced between.

RIGHT FRONT
Cast on 36 (37: 38: 40: 41: 43) sts using 10mm (US 15) needles.
Row 1 (WS): K10 (11: 12: 14: 15: 17), place marker on right needle, K8, place marker on right needle, K18.
Now work in patt as folls:
Row 1 (RS): K to marker, slip marker onto right needle, yfwd, K8, yfwd, slip marker onto right needle, K to end.
Row 2: K0 (0: 1: 0: 0: 2), P0 (1: 1: 0: 1: 1), (K3, P1) 2 (2: 2: 3: 3: 3) times, K2, slip marker onto right needle, K1, P8, K1, slip marker onto right needle, K2, (P1, K3) 4 times.
Row 3: K to marker, slip marker onto right needle, K1, yfwd, K8, yfwd, K1, slip marker onto right needle, K to end.
Row 4: K1 (2: 0: 1: 2: 0), P1 (1: 0: 1: 1: 1), (K3, P1) 2 (2: 3: 3: 3: 4) times, slip marker onto right needle, K2, P8, K2, slip marker onto right needle, (P1, K3) 3 times, P1, K5.
Row 5: K to marker, slip marker onto right needle, K2, yfwd, K8, yfwd, K2, slip marker onto right needle, K to end.
Row 6: K0 (0: 1: 0: 0: 2), P0 (1: 1: 0: 1: 1), (K3, P1) 2 (2: 2: 3: 3: 3) times, K2, slip marker onto right needle, K1, P1, K1, P8, K1, P1, K1, slip marker onto right needle, K2, (P1, K3) 4 times.
Row 7: K to marker, slip marker onto right needle, K3, K4tog tbl, K4tog, K3, slip marker onto right needle, K to end.
Row 8: K1 (2: 0: 1: 2: 0), P1 (1: 0: 1: 1: 1), (K3, P1) 2 (2: 3: 3: 3: 4) times, slip marker onto right needle, K8, slip marker onto right needle, (P1, K3) 3 times, P1, K5.

These 8 rows form patt.
Cont in patt, shaping side seam by dec 1 st at end of 13th and foll 8th row.
34 (35: 36: 38: 39: 41) sts.
Work 7 rows, ending with a WS row.
Row 37 (buttonhole row) (RS): K2, K2tog tbl, yfwd (to make first buttonhole of first pair), K10, yfwd, K2tog (to make 2nd buttonhole of first pair), K to last 2 sts, K2tog.
Working a further 4 pairs of button-holes in this way to correspond with positions marked for buttons on left front and noting that no further reference will be made to buttonholes, complete to match left front, reversing shapings and working first row of neck shaping as folls:

Shape front neck
Next row (RS): Patt 13 sts and slip these sts onto a holder, patt to end.
15 (15: 16: 16: 17: 17) sts.

SLEEVES (both alike)
Cast on 23 (25: 25: 27: 27: 29) sts using 10mm (US 15) needles.
Work in patt as folls:
Row 1 (RS): Knit.
Row 2: K3 (0: 0: 1: 1: 2), *P1, K3, rep from * to last 0 (1: 1: 2: 2: 3) sts, P0 (1: 1: 1: 1: 1), K0 (0: 0: 1: 1: 2).
Row 3: Knit.
Row 4: K1 (2: 2: 3: 3: 0), *P1, K3, rep from * to last 2 (3: 3: 0: 0: 1) sts, P1 (1: 1: 0: 0: 1), K1 (2: 2: 0: 0: 0).
These 4 rows form patt.

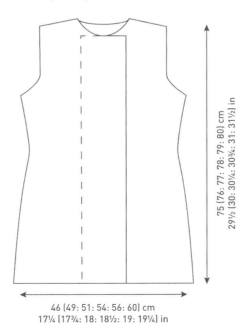

75 (76: 77: 78: 79: 80) cm
29½ (30: 30¼: 30¾: 31: 31½) in

46 (49: 51: 54: 56: 60) cm
17¼ (17¾: 18: 18½: 19: 19¼) in

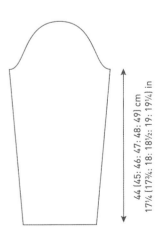

44 (45: 46: 47: 48: 49) cm
17¼ (17¾: 18: 18½: 19: 19¼) in

Continued on next page...

Recommendation
Suitable for the knitter with a little experience
Please see pages 23 & 34 for photographs.

One size
Rowan Big Wool
      1   x 100gm
Photographed in Concrete and Glum

Needles
1 pair 10mm (no 000) (US 15) needles

Tension
10 sts and 15 rows to 10 cm measured over
pattern using 10mm (US 15) needles.

EDEN
TEXTURED CLOSE FITTING HAT

HAT
Cast on 37 sts using 10mm (US 15) needles.
Row 1 (RS): Purl.
Row 2: Knit.
Row 3: K1, *yfwd, K8, yfwd, K1, rep from * to
end. 45 sts.
Row 4: K1, *K1, P8, K2, rep from * to end.
Row 5: K1, *K1, yfwd, K8, yfwd, K2, rep from *
to end. 53 sts.
Row 6: K1, *K2, P8, K3, rep from * to end.
Row 7: K1, *K2, yfwd, K8, yfwd, K3, rep from *
to end. 61 sts.
Row 8: K1, *K3, P8, K4, rep from * to end.
Row 9: K1, *K3, K4tog tbl, K4tog, K4, rep from
* to end. 37 sts.
Row 10: Knit.
Rows 11 to 18: As rows 3 to 8.
Row 19: K2tog, K to end. 36 sts.
Row 20: Knit.
Shape top
Row 1 (RS): (K3, K2tog) 7 times, K1. 29 sts.
Rows 2 to 4: Knit.
Row 5: (K2, K2tog) 7 times, K1. 22 sts.

Row 6: Knit.
Row 7: (K1, K2tog) 7 times, K1. 15 sts.
Row 8: Knit.
Row 9: (K2tog) 7 times, K1.
Break yarn and thread through rem 8 sts.
Pull up tight and fasten off securely.
Join back seam.

FOREST – *Continued from previous page.*

Cont in patt, shaping sides by inc 1 st at each
end of 9th (9th: 9th: 11th: 7th: 7th) and every
foll 14th (14th: 16th: 16th: 12th: 12th) row to
29 (29: 33: 35: 33: 33) sts, then on every foll
16th (16th: -: -: 14th: 14th) row until there are
31 (33: -: -: 37: 39) sts, taking inc sts into patt.
Cont straight until sleeve measures 44 (45:
46: 47: 48: 49) cm, ending with a WS row.
Shape top
Keeping patt correct, cast off 3 sts at beg
of next 2 rows. 25 (27: 27: 29: 31: 33) sts.
Dec 1 st at each end of next and 3 foll 4th
rows, then on every foll alt row to 13 sts,
then on foll row, ending with a WS row.
Cast off rem 11 sts.

MAKING UP
Press all pieces with a warm iron over a
damp cloth.
Join both shoulder seams using back stitch
or mattress stitch if preferred.

Neckband
With RS facing and using 9mm (US 13)
needles, slip 13 sts from right front holder
onto right needle, rejoin yarn and pick up
and knit 10 (10: 10: 12: 12: 12) sts up right
side of neck, 15 (15: 15: 17: 17: 17) sts from
back, and 10 (10: 10: 12: 12: 12) sts down
left side of neck, then K across 13 sts on left
front holder. 61 (61: 61: 67: 67: 67) sts.
Cast off knitwise (on **WS**).
Sleeve tabs (make 2)
Cast on 5 sts using 9mm (US 13) needles.
Work in g st for 34 rows.
Cast off.
Epaulettes (make 2)
Cast on 5 sts using 9mm (US 13) needles.
Work in g st for 20 rows.
Cast off.
Lay epaulette over shoulder seam so that
cast-off edge matches armhole edge and
sew in place at armhole edge.

Join side seams.
Join sleeve seams, enclosing cast-off end
of sleeve tab in sleeve seam - position tab
5 cm up from sleeve cast-on edge.
Sew sleeves into armholes, enclosing end
of epaulette in seam.
Sew on buttons, attach one to each sleeve
tab as in photograph to secure tabs in place,
and one to end of each epaulette to secure
in place.
Make button loop at top edge of right front
border, then sew on small button to left front
to correspond.
Repeat on inside of left front border, sewing
on small button to inside of right front.
Join side seams. Join sleeve seams, enclosing
cast-off end of sleeve tab in sleeve seam -
position tab 5 cm up from sleeve cast-on edge.
Sew sleeves into armholes.
Sew on buttons, attach one to each sleeve tab
as in photograph to secure tabs in place.

ISLE

DOUBLE BREASTED CARDIGAN FEATURING BOX PLEATS

Recommendation
Suitable for the knitter with a little experience
Please see pages 34 & 35 for photographs.

	XS	S	M	L	XL	XXL	
To fit	81	86	91	97	102	109	cm
bust	32	34	36	38	40	43	in

Rowan Baby Alpaca DK

| | 11 | 12 | 12 | 13 | 13 | 14 | x 50gm |

Photographed in Southdown

Needles
1 pair 3mm (no 11) (US 2/3) needles
1 pair 3¼mm (no 10) (US 3) needles

Buttons – 12 Medium
6 Small

Tension
24 sts and 33 rows to 10 cm measured over
stocking stitch using 3¼mm (US 3) needles.

Pattern note: While working pleats, slip all sts
purlwise with yarn held at back of work - this
is WS of work on RS rows, and RS of work on
WS rows.

BACK
Cast on 175 (181: 187: 193: 199: 209) sts
using 3¼mm (US 3) needles.
Row 1 (RS): K26 (28: 30: 32: 34: 37), sl
1 (see pattern note), P34, sl 1, K51 (53: 55:
57: 59: 63), sl 1, P34, sl 1, K26 (28: 30: 32:
34: 37).
Row 2: K27 (29: 31: 33: 35: 38), *P8, sl 1
and place marker on this st, P16, sl 1 and
place marker on this st, P8*, K53 (55: 57:
59: 61: 65), rep from * to * once more, K27
(29: 31: 33: 35: 38).
(4 markers on needle.)
Row 3: As row 1.
Row 4: K27 (29: 31: 33: 35: 38), *P8, sl
marked st, P16, sl marked st, P8*, K53 (55:
57: 59: 61: 65), rep from * to * once more,
K27 (29: 31: 33: 35: 38).
Row 5: As row 1.
Row 6: P27 (29: 31: 33: 35: 38), *K8, sl
marked st, K16, sl marked st, K8*, P53 (55:
57: 59: 61: 65), rep from * to * once more,
P27 (29: 31: 33: 35: 38).
Last 2 rows form patt.
Keeping patt correct, cont as folls:
Work 4 rows.
Row 11 (RS): K3, K2tog (for side seam dec),
(patt to within 2 sts of marked st, P2tog, P
marked st, P2tog tbl) 4 times, patt to last 5 sts,
K2tog tbl (for side seam dec), K3.
165 (171: 177: 183: 189: 199) sts.
Work 7 rows.
Row 19: As row 11.
155 (161: 167: 173: 179: 189) sts.
Work 5 rows.
Row 25: As row 11.
145 (151: 157: 163: 169: 179) sts.
Work 3 rows.
Row 29: As row 11.
135 (141: 147: 153: 159: 169) sts.
Work 3 rows.
Row 33: As row 11.
125 (131: 137: 143: 149: 159) sts.
Row 34: P21 (23: 25: 27: 29: 32), cast off
next 16 sts, P until there are 51 (53: 55: 57:
59: 63) sts on right needle after cast-off, cast
off next 16 sts, P to end.
93 (99: 105: 111: 117: 127) sts.
Cast-off sts form tops of pleats and will be
folded into position later.

Now working all sts in st st, beg with a K row,
cont as folls:
Work 2 rows, ending with a WS row.
Working side seam decreases as set, dec 1 st
at each end of next row.
91 (97: 103: 109: 115: 125) sts.
Work 19 rows, ending with a WS row.
Next row (inc) (RS): K3, M1, K to last 3 sts,
M1, K3.
Working all side seam increases as set by last
row, inc 1 st at each end of 10th and 4 foll
10th rows.
103 (109: 115: 121: 127: 137) sts.
Cont straight until back measures 35 (35: 36:
36: 36: 36) cm, ending with a WS row.
Shape armholes
Cast off 3 (4: 4: 5: 5: 6) sts at beg of next
2 rows. 97 (101: 107: 111: 117: 125) sts.
Dec 1 st at each end of next 5 (5: 7: 7: 9: 9)
rows, then on foll 4 (5: 5: 6: 6: 8) alt rows,
then on foll 4th row.
77 (79: 81: 83: 85: 89) sts.
Cont straight until armhole measures 18 (19:
19: 20: 21: 22) cm, ending with a WS row.
Shape back neck and shoulders
Cast off 7 (7: 7: 7: 7: 8) sts at beg of next
2 rows. 63 (65: 67: 69: 71: 73) sts.
Next row (RS): Cast off 7 (7: 7: 7: 7: 8) sts,
K until there are 10 (10: 11: 11: 12: 12) sts on
right needle and turn, leaving rem sts on
a holder.
Work each side of neck separately.
Cast off 4 sts at beg of next row.
Cast off rem 6 (6: 7: 7: 8: 8) sts.
With RS facing, rejoin yarn to rem sts, cast off
centre 29 (31: 31: 33: 33: 33) sts, K to end.
Complete to match first side, reversing
shapings.

LEFT FRONT
Cast on 105 (108: 111: 114: 117: 122) sts
using 3¼mm (US 3) needles.
Row 1 (RS): K26 (28: 30: 32: 34: 37), sl 1,
P34, sl 1, K20 (21: 22: 23: 24: 26), (P1, K1)
9 times, P1, K4.
Row 2: K4, P1, (K1 P1) 9 times, 21 (22: 23:
24: 25: 27), P8, sl 1 and place marker on this
st, P16, sl 1 and place marker on this st, P8,
K27 (29: 31: 33: 35: 38).
(2 markers on needle.)

Row 3: As row 1.
Row 4: K4, P1, (K1, P1) 9 times, K21 (22: 23: 24: 25: 27), P8, sl marked st, P16, sl marked st, P8, K27 (29: 31: 33: 35: 38).
Row 5: As row 1.
Row 6: K4, P1, (K1, P1) 9 times, K4, P17 (18: 19: 20: 21: 23), K8, sl marked st, K16, sl marked st, K8, P27 (29: 31: 33: 35: 38).
Last 2 rows form patt.
Keeping patt correct, cont as folls:
Work 4 rows.
Row 11 (RS): K3, K2tog (for side seam dec), (patt to within 2 sts of marked st, P2tog, P marked st, P2tog tbl) twice, patt to end.
100 (103: 106: 109: 112: 117) sts.
Work 7 rows.
Row 19: As row 11.
95 (98: 101: 104: 107: 112) sts.
Work 5 rows.
Row 25: As row 11.
90 (93: 96: 99: 102: 107) sts.
Work 3 rows.
Row 29: As row 11.
85 (88: 91: 94: 97: 102) sts.
Work 3 rows.
Row 33: As row 11.
80 (83: 86: 89: 92: 97) sts.
Row 34: Patt 43 (44: 45: 46: 47: 49) sts, cast off next 16 sts, P to end.
64 (67: 70: 73: 76: 81) sts.
Cast-off sts form top of pleat and will be folded into position later.
Now working all sts above pleat in st st, beg with a K row, and keeping front opening edge 27 sts in patt as set, cont as folls:
Work 2 rows, ending with a WS row.
Working side seam decreases as set, dec 1 st at beg of next row. 63 (66: 69: 72: 75: 80) sts.
Work 19 rows, ending with a WS row.
Working all side seam increases as set by back, inc 1 st at beg of next and 5 foll 10th rows. 69 (72: 75: 78: 81: 86) sts.
Cont straight until left front matches back to beg of armhole shaping, ending with a WS row.
Shape armhole
Keeping patt correct, cast off 3 (4: 4: 5: 5: 6) sts at beg of next row.
66 (68: 71: 73: 76: 80) sts.
Work 1 row.
Dec 1 st at armhole edge of next 5 (5: 7: 7: 9: 9) rows, then on foll 4 (5: 5: 6: 6: 8) alt rows, then on foll 4th row.
56 (57: 58: 59: 60: 62) sts.
Cont straight until 18 (18: 18: 20: 20: 20) rows less have been worked than on back to beg of shoulder shaping, ending with a WS row.

Shape front neck
Next row (RS): K28 (28: 29: 30: 31: 33) and turn, leaving rem 28 (29: 29: 29: 29: 29) sts on a holder.
Dec 1 st at neck edge of next 4 rows, then on foll 3 (3: 3: 4: 4: 4) alt rows, then on foll 4th row.
20 (20: 21: 21: 22: 24) sts.
Work 3 rows, ending with a WS row.
Shape shoulder
Cast off 7 (7: 7: 7: 7: 8) sts at beg of next and foll alt row.
Work 1 row.
Cast off rem 6 (6: 7: 7: 8: 8) sts.
Mark positions for 6 pairs of buttons along left front opening edge - first pair of buttons to come in row 23, top pair of buttons to come 1.5 cm below neck shaping, and rem 4 pairs of buttons evenly spaced between.

RIGHT FRONT
Cast on 105 (108: 111: 114: 117: 122) sts using 3¼mm (US 3) needles.
Row 1 (RS): K4, (P1, K1) 9 times, P1, K20 (21: 22: 23: 24: 26), sl 1, P34, sl 1, K26 (28: 30: 32: 34: 37).
Row 2: K27 (29: 31: 33: 35: 38), P8, sl 1 and place marker on this st, P16, sl 1 and place marker on this st, P8, K21 (22: 23: 24: 25: 27), P1, (K1, P1) 9 times, K4.
(2 markers on needle.)
Row 3: As row 1.
Row 4: K27 (29: 31: 33: 35: 38), P8, sl marked st, P16, sl marked st, P8, K21 (22: 23: 24: 25: 27), P1, (K1, P1) 9 times, K4.
Row 5: As row 1.
Row 6: P27 (29: 31: 33: 35: 38), K8, sl marked st, K16, sl marked st, K8, P17 (18: 19: 20: 21: 23), K4, P1, (K1, P1) 9 times, K4.
Last 2 rows form patt.
Keeping patt correct, cont as folls:
Work 4 rows.
Row 11 (RS): (Patt to within 2 sts of marked st, P2tog, P marked st, P2tog tbl) twice, patt to last 5 sts, K2tog tbl (for side seam dec), K3.
100 (103: 106: 109: 112: 117) sts.
Work 7 rows.
Row 19: As row 11.
95 (98: 101: 104: 107: 112) sts.
Work 3 rows.
Row 23 (buttonhole row) (RS): K4, P2tog tbl, (yon) twice, K2tog (to make first buttonhole of first pair - work twice into double yon on next row), patt 11 sts, K2tog tbl, (yon) twice, P2tog (to make 2nd buttonhole of first pair - work twice into double yon on next row), patt to end.

Working a further 5 pairs of buttonholes in this way to correspond with positions marked for buttons on left front and noting that no further reference will be made to buttonholes, cont as folls:
Work 1 row.
Row 25: As row 11.
90 (93: 96: 99: 102: 107) sts.
Work 3 rows.
Row 29: As row 11.
85 (88: 91: 94: 97: 102) sts.
Work 3 rows.
Row 33: As row 11.
80 (83: 86: 89: 92: 97) sts.
Row 34: P21 (23: 25: 27: 29: 32), cast off next 16 sts, patt to end.
64 (67: 70: 73: 76: 81) sts.
Cast-off sts form top of pleat and will be folded into position later.
Now working all sts above pleat in st st, beg with a K row, and keeping front opening edge 27 sts in patt as set, cont as folls:
Work 2 rows, ending with a WS row.
Working side seam decreases as set, dec 1 st at end of next row. 63 (66: 69: 72: 75: 80) sts.
Complete to match left front, reversing shapings and working first row of neck shaping as folls:
Shape front neck
Next row (RS): Patt 28 (29: 29: 29: 29: 29) sts and slip these sts onto a holder, patt to end. 28 (28: 29: 30: 31: 33) sts.

LEFT SLEEVE
Front sleeve
Cast on 39 (40: 41: 42: 43: 44) sts using 3mm (US 2/3) needles.
Row 1 (RS): K5, *P1, K1, rep from * to last 0 (1: 0: 1: 0: 1) st, P0 (1: 0: 1: 0: 1).
Row 2: P0 (1: 0: 1: 0: 1), *K1, P1, rep from * to last 5 sts, K5.
These 2 rows set the sts.
Cont as set, inc 1 st at end of 11th and foll 10th row. 41 (42: 43: 44: 45: 46) sts.
Work 7 rows, ending with a WS row.
Break yarn and leave sts on a holder.
Back sleeve
Cast on 13 (14: 15: 16: 17: 18) sts using 3mm (US 2/3) needles.
Row 1 (RS): P0 (1: 0: 1: 0: 1), *K1, P1, rep from * to last 5 sts, K5.
Row 2: K5, *P1, K1, rep from * to last 0 (1: 0: 1: 0: 1) st, P0 (1: 0: 1: 0: 1).
These 2 rows set the sts.
Cont as set, inc 1 st at beg of 11th and foll 10th row. 15 (16: 17: 18: 19: 20) sts.
Work 7 rows, ending with a WS row.

Join sections

Change to 3¼mm (US 3) needles.

Next row (RS): K to last 5 sts of back sleeve, holding WS of front sleeve against RS of back sleeve K tog first st of front sleeve with next st of back sleeve, (K tog next st of front sleeve with next st of back sleeve) 4 times, K rem 36 (37: 38: 39: 40: 41) sts of front sleeve. 51 (53: 55: 57: 59: 61) sts.

**Beg with a P row and working all sleeve increases in same way as side seam increases, cont in st st, shaping sides by inc 1 st at each end of 2nd (2nd: 2nd: 2nd: 2nd: 4th) and every foll 10th (10th: 10th: 10th: 12th: 12th) row to 69 (67: 65: 65: 81: 83) sts, then on every foll 12th (12th: 12th: 12th: -: -) row until there are 73 (75: 77: 79: -: -) sts.

Cont straight until sleeve measures 44 (45: 46: 47: 48: 49) cm, ending with a WS row.

Shape top

Cast off 3 (4: 4: 5: 5: 6) sts at beg of next 2 rows. 67 (67: 69: 69: 71: 71) sts.

Dec 1 st at each end of next 3 rows, then on foll alt row, then on 6 (7: 6: 7: 7: 8) foll 4th rows. 47 (45: 49: 47: 49: 47) sts.

Work 1 row, ending with a WS row.

Dec 1 st at each end of next and foll 3 (2: 4: 3: 4: 3) alt rows, then on foll 5 rows, ending with a WS row.

Cast off rem 29 sts.

RIGHT SLEEVE
Back sleeve

Cast on 13 (14: 15: 16: 17: 18) sts using 3mm (US 2/3) needles.

Row 1 (RS): K5, *P1, K1, rep from * to last 0 (1: 0: 1: 0: 1) st, P0 (1: 0: 1: 0: 1).

Row 2: P0 (1: 0: 1: 0: 1), *K1, P1, rep from * to last 5 sts, K5.

These 2 rows set the sts.

Cont as set, inc 1 st at end of 11th and foll 10th row.

15 (16: 17: 18: 19: 20) sts.

Work 7 rows, ending with a WS row.

Break yarn and leave sts on a holder.

Front sleeve

Cast on 39 (40: 41: 42: 43: 44) sts using 3mm (US 2/3) needles.

Row 1 (RS): P0 (1: 0: 1: 0: 1), *K1, P1, rep from * to last 5 sts, K5.

Row 2: K5, *P1, K1, rep from * to last 0 (1: 0: 1: 0: 1) st, P0 (1: 0: 1: 0: 1).

These 2 rows set the sts.

Cont as set, inc 1 st at beg of 11th and foll 10th row. 41 (42: 43: 44: 45: 46) sts.

Work 7 rows, ending with a WS row.

Join sections

Change to 3¼mm (US 3) needles.

Next row (RS): K to last 5 sts of front sleeve, holding WS of front sleeve against RS of back sleeve K tog next st of front sleeve with first st of back sleeve, (K tog next st of front sleeve with next st of back sleeve) 4 times, K rem 10 (11: 12: 13: 14: 15) sts of back sleeve. 51 (53: 55: 57: 59: 61) sts.

Complete as given for left sleeve from **.

MAKING UP

Press all pieces with a warm iron over a damp cloth.

Join both shoulder seams using back stitch or mattress stitch if preferred.

Neckband

With RS facing and using 3mm (US 2/3) needles, slip 28 (29: 29: 29: 29: 29) sts from right front holder onto right needle, rejoin yarn and pick up and knit 22 (22: 22: 24: 24: 24) sts up right side of neck, 37 (39: 39: 41: 41: 41) sts from back, and 22 (22: 22: 24: 24: 24) sts down left side of neck, then patt across 28 (29: 29: 29: 29: 29) sts on left front holder. 137 (141: 141: 147: 147: 147) sts.

Row 1 (WS): Patt 27 sts, K to last 27 sts, patt 27 sts.

Rep this row 3 times more, ending with a **RS** row.

Cast off in patt (on **WS**).

Using photograph as a guide, fold pleats along slip st fold lines and sew cast-off edge in place on inside at top of pleat. Join side seams. Join sleeve seams. Sew sleeves into armholes. Sew on buttons, attaching 3 to each sleeve opening as in photograph.

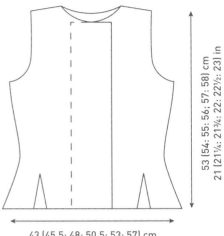

53 (54: 55: 56: 57: 58) cm
21 (21¼: 21¼: 21¾: 22: 22½: 23) in

43 (45.5: 48: 50.5: 53: 57) cm
17 (18: 19: 20: 21: 22½) in

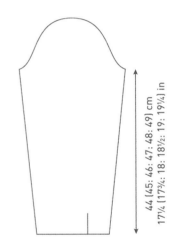

44 (45: 46: 47: 48: 49) cm
17¼ (17¾: 18: 18½: 19: 19¼) in

Recommendation

Suitable for the knitter with a little experience
Please see pages 30 & 31 for photographs.

	XS	S	M	L	XL	XXL	
To fit	**81**	**86**	**91**	**97**	**102**	**109**	cm
bust	32	34	36	38	40	43	in

Rowan Kidsilk Aura

4   5   5   6   6   7   x 25gm

Photographed in Cypress

Needles

1 pair 7mm (no 2) (US 10½) needles
1 pair 8mm (no 0) (US 11) needles

Tension

11 sts and 15 rows to 10 cm measured over
stocking stitch using 8mm (US 11) needles.

BOUNTY
NEAT SHRUG WITH FRONT TIES

BACK
Cast on 36 (38: 40: 44: 46: 50) sts using
7mm (US 10½) needles.
Work in g st for 6 rows, ending with a
WS row.
Beg with a K row, now work in st st
throughout as folls:
Work 2 rows.
Change to 8mm (US 11) needles.
Next row (inc) (RS): K2, M1, K to last 2 sts,
M1, K2.
Working all side seam increases as set by last
row, inc 1 st at each end of 4th and 2 foll 4th
rows. 44 (46: 48: 52: 54: 58) sts.
Work 3 rows, ending with a WS row.
(Back should measure 16 cm.)
Shape armholes
Cast off 2 sts at beg of next 2 rows.
40 (42: 44: 48: 50: 54) sts.
Dec 1 st at each end of next 3 (3: 3: 5: 5: 7) rows,
then on foll alt row. 32 (34: 36: 36: 38: 38) sts.
Work 17 (19: 21: 21: 21: 21) rows, ending
with a WS row.
Shape back neck and shoulders
Next row (RS): K10 (11: 12: 11: 12: 12)
and turn, leaving rem sts on a holder.
Work each side of neck separately.
Dec 1 st at neck edge of next 3 rows **and
at same time** cast off 3 (4: 4: 4: 4: 4) sts
at beg of 2nd row.
Cast off rem 4 (4: 5: 4: 5: 5) sts.
With RS facing, rejoin yarn to rem sts,
cast off centre 12 (12: 12: 14: 14: 14) sts,
K to end.
Complete to match first side, reversing
shapings.

LEFT FRONT
Cast on 64 (65: 66: 68: 69: 71) sts using
7mm (US 10½) needles.
Work in g st for 7 rows, dec 1 st at beg of
2nd row and at same edge on foll 5 rows
and ending with a **RS** row.
58 (59: 60: 62: 63: 65) sts.
Row 8 (WS): Cast off 34 sts, P to end.
24 (25: 26: 28: 29: 31) sts.
Change to 8mm (US 11) needles.
Row 9 (inc) (RS): K2, M1 (for side seam inc),
K to last 7 sts, K2tog (for front slope dec), K to
last st, pick up loop lying between needles and

place this loop on right needle (**note**: this loop
does **NOT** count as a st), sl last st purlwise.
24 (25: 26: 28: 29: 31) sts.
Row 10: P tog first st and the picked-up loop,
P to end.
Last 2 rows set the sts - st st with slip st
edging up front opening edge, front slope
decreases worked 7 sts in from front opening
edge and side seam increases worked as given
for back.
Keeping sts correct as now set, cont as folls:
Dec 1 st at front slope edge of 3rd and 2 foll
4th rows **and at same time** inc 1 st at side
seam edge of 3rd and 2 foll 4th rows.
24 (25: 26: 28: 29: 31) sts.
Work 3 rows, ending with a WS row.
Shape armholes
Cast off 2 sts at beg and dec 1 st at front slope
edge of next row. 21 (22: 23: 25: 26: 28) sts.
Work 1 row.
Dec 1 st at armhole edge of next 3 (3: 3: 5: 5:
7) rows, then on foll alt row and at same time
dec 1 st at front slope edge of 3rd and 0 (0: 0:
1: 1: 1) foll 4th row. 16 (17: 18: 17: 18: 18) sts.
Dec 1 st at front slope edge only on 2nd (2nd:
2nd: 4th: 4th: 2nd) and 3 (2: 1: 2: 2: 1) foll
4th rows, then on 0 (1: 2: 1: 1: 2) foll 6th rows.
12 (13: 14: 13: 14: 14) sts.
Work 5 rows, ending with a WS row.
Shape shoulder
Cast off 3 (4: 4: 4: 4: 4) sts at beg of next row,
then 4 (4: 5: 4: 5: 5) sts at beg of foll alt row.
5 sts.
Cont as set on rem 5 sts only (for back neck
border extension) for a further 8 (8: 8: 9: 9: 9)
cm, ending with a WS row.
Cast off.

RIGHT FRONT
Cast on 64 (65: 66: 68: 69: 71) sts using
7mm (US 10½) needles.
Note: This front is a mirror reflection of left
front. Rather than working shaping at opposite
ends of rows as would be the usual way, this
front is reversed by reversing RS of work.
Row 1 (WS): Purl.
Row 2: P2tog, P to end.
Row 3: P to last 2 sts, P2tog.
Rows 4 to 7: As rows 2 and 3, twice.
58 (59: 60: 62: 63: 65) sts.

Row 8 (RS): Cast off 34 sts, K to end.
24 (25: 26: 28: 29: 31) sts.
Change to 8mm (US 11) needles.
Row 9 (inc) (WS): P2, M1P (for side seam inc),
P to last 7 sts, P2tog (for front slope dec), P to
last st, pick up loop lying between needles and
place this loop on right needle (**note**: this loop
does **NOT** count as a st), sl last st purlwise.
24 (25: 26: 28: 29: 31) sts.
Row 10: K tog tbl first st and the picked-up
loop, K to end.
Last 2 rows set the sts - st st with slip st
edging up front opening edge, front slope
decreases worked 7 sts in from front opening
edge and side seam increases.
Keeping sts correct as now set, complete as
given for left front, reversing all shaping by
reading K for P (and vice versa), and RS for
WS (and vice versa).

SLEEVES (both alike)

Cast on 19 (21: 23: 23: 25: 25) sts using
8mm (US 11) needles.
Beg with a K row, work in st st throughout
as folls:
Work 12 (12: 12: 12: 14: 14) rows, ending
with a WS row.
Next row (inc) (RS): K2, M1, K to last 2 sts,
M1, K2.
Working all increases as set by last row,
inc 1 st at each end of 12th (12th: 12th:
14th: 14th: 14th) and 1 (1: 0: 0: 0: 0) foll
12th row, then on every foll 14th row until
there are 29 (31: 33: 33: 35: 35) sts.
Cont straight until sleeve measures 47 (48:
49: 50: 51: 52) cm, ending with a WS row.

Shape top
Cast off 2 sts at beg of next 2 rows.
25 (27: 29: 29: 31: 31) sts.
Dec 1 st at each end of next and foll alt row,
then on foll 4th row.
19 (21: 23: 23: 25: 25) sts.
Work 3 rows, ending with a WS row.
Dec 1 st at each end of next and every foll alt
row to 15 sts, then on foll 3 rows, ending with
a WS row.
Cast off rem 9 sts.

MAKING UP

Press all pieces with a warm iron over a damp
cloth.
Join both shoulder seams using back stitch or
mattress stitch if preferred. Join cast-off ends
of back neck border extensions, then sew one
edge to back neck edge. Join side seams. Join
sleeve seams. Sew sleeves into armholes.

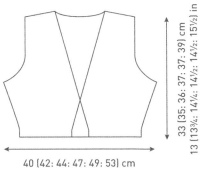

33 (35: 36: 37: 37: 39) cm
13 (13¾: 14¼: 14½: 14½: 15½) in

40 (42: 44: 47: 49: 53) cm
15¾ (16½: 17½: 18½: 19½: 21) in

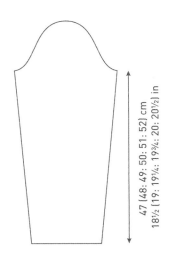

47 (48: 49: 50: 51: 52) cm
18½ (19: 19¼: 19¾: 20: 20½) in

LUNA

Recommendation

Suitable for the more experienced knitter
Please see pages 24 & 25 for photographs.

	XS	S	M	L	XL	XXL	
To fit	81	86	91	97	102	109	cm
bust	32	34	36	38	40	43	in

Rowan Kidsilk Haze

| | 5 | 5 | 6 | 6 | 7 | 7 | x 25gm |

Photographed in Majestic

Needles

1 pair 2¾mm (no 12) (US 2) needles
1 pair 3¼mm (no 10) (US 3) needles

Buttons – 7

Beads – approx. 490 (520: 550: 580: 610: 650) small glass beads

Tension

25 sts and 34 rows to 10 cm measured over stocking stitch using 3¼mm (US 3) needles.

Special abbreviation

MP = make picot as folls: cast on 1 st, then cast off 1 st.

Beading note: Before starting to knit, thread beads onto yarn. To do this, thread a fine sewing needle (one you will easily pass through the beads) with sewing thread. Knot ends of thread and then pass end of yarn through this loop. Thread a bead onto sewing thread and then gently slide it along and onto knitting yarn. Continue in this way until required number of beads are on yarn.

BACK

Thread 195 (207: 219: 231: 243: 261) beads onto yarn.
Using 3¼mm (US 3) needles, work beaded cast on as folls: *cast on 1 st, slide bead up next to st on left needle, cast on 1 st, rep from * until there are 390 (414: 438: 462: 486: 522) sts on needle.
Row 1 (RS): *K2, lift 2nd st on right needle over first st and off right needle, rep from * to end. 195 (207: 219: 231: 243: 261) sts.
Row 2: Knit.
Row 3: K1, (K1, yfwd, K1) into next st, (K1 wrapping yarn round needle twice) 5 times, *(K1, yfwd, K1, yfwd, K1) into next st, (K1 wrapping yarn round needle twice) 5 times, rep from * to last 2 sts, (K1, yfwd, K1) into next st, K1.
Row 4: K4, slip next 5 sts onto right needle dropping extra loops, slip same 5 sts back onto left needle and P these 5 sts tog, *K5, slip next 5 sts onto right needle dropping extra loops, slip same 5 sts back onto left needle and P these 5 sts tog, rep from * to last 4 sts, K4.
Row 5: Knit.
Row 6: Purl.
Row 7: K1, (K1 wrapping yarn round needle twice) 3 times, (K1, yfwd, K1, yfwd, K1) into next st, *(K1 wrapping yarn round needle twice) 5 times, (K1, yfwd, K1, yfwd, K1) into next st, rep from * to last 4 sts, (K1 wrapping yarn round needle twice) 3 times, K1.
Row 8: K1, slip next 3 sts onto right needle dropping extra loops, slip same 3 sts back onto left needle and P these 3 sts tog, K5, *slip next 5 sts onto right needle dropping extra loops, slip same 5 sts back onto left needle and P these 5 sts tog, K5, rep from * to last 4 sts, slip next 3 sts onto right needle dropping extra loops, slip same 3 sts back onto left needle and P these 3 sts tog, K1.
These 8 rows complete lace border.
Beg with a K row, work in st st for 18 rows, dec 3 (3: 3: 3: 3: 1) sts evenly across first of these rows and ending with a WS row.
192 (204: 216: 228: 240: 260) sts.
Row 27 (RS): *K2tog, rep from * to end.
96 (102: 108: 114: 120: 130) sts.
Place markers at both ends of last row.
Work 11 rows, ending with a WS row.

Next row (inc) (RS): K3, M1, K to last 3 sts, M1, K3. 98 (104: 110: 116: 122: 132) sts.
Working all side seam increases as set by last row, inc 1 st at each end of 12th and 4 foll 10th rows. 108 (114: 120: 126: 132: 142) sts.
Cont straight until back measures 23 (23: 24: 24: 24: 24) cm from markers, end with a WS row.
Shape raglan armholes
Cast off 5 sts at beg of next 2 rows.
98 (104: 110: 116: 122: 132) sts.
Sizes XS and S only
Work 2 rows.
Sizes M, L, XL and XXL only
Next row (RS): K1, K2tog, K to last 3 sts, K2tog tbl, K1.
Next row: P1, P2tog tbl, P to last 3 sts, P2tog, P1.
Rep last 2 rows - (-: 1: 1: 2: 5) times more.
- (-: 102: 108: 110: 108) sts.
All sizes
Next row (RS): K1, K2tog, K to last 3 sts, K2tog tbl, K1.
Next row: Purl.
Rep last 2 rows 24 (26: 25: 27: 28: 27) times more, ending with a WS row.
Cast off rem 48 (50: 50: 52: 52: 52) sts.

LEFT FRONT

Thread 103 (109: 115: 121: 127: 139) beads onto yarn.
Using 3¼mm (US 3) needles, work beaded cast on as folls: *cast on 1 st, slide bead up next to st on left needle, cast on 1 st, rep from * until there are 206 (218: 230: 242: 254: 278) sts on needle.
Row 1 (RS): *K2, lift 2nd st on right needle over first st and off right needle, rep from * to end.
103 (109: 115: 121: 127: 139) sts.
Row 2: Knit.**
Row 3: K1, (K1, yfwd, K1) into next st, (K1 wrapping yarn round needle twice) 5 times, *(K1, yfwd, K1, yfwd, K1) into next st, (K1 wrapping yarn round needle twice) 5 times, rep from * to last 6 sts, (K1, yfwd, K1) into next st, K5.
Row 4: MP, K until there are 8 sts on right needle, slip next 5 sts onto right needle dropping extra loops, slip same 5 sts back onto left needle and P these 5 sts tog, *K5, slip next 5 sts onto right needle dropping extra loops, slip same 5 sts back onto left needle and P these 5 sts tog, rep from * to last 4 sts, K4.

Row 5: Knit.
Row 6: K5, P to end.
Row 7: K1, (K1 wrapping yarn round needle twice) 3 times, (K1, yfwd, K1, yfwd, K1) into next st, *(K1 wrapping yarn round needle twice) 5 times, (K1, yfwd, K1, yfwd, K1) into next st, rep from * to last 8 sts, (K1 wrapping yarn round needle twice) 3 times, K5.
Row 8: MP, K until there are 5 sts on right needle, slip next 3 sts onto right needle dropping extra loops, slip same 3 sts back onto left needle and P these 3 sts tog, K5, *slip next 5 sts onto right needle dropping extra loops, slip same 5 sts back onto left needle and P these 5 sts tog, K5, rep from * to last 4 sts, slip next 3 sts onto right needle dropping extra loops, slip same 3 sts back onto left needle and P these 3 sts tog, K1. These 8 rows complete lace border.
Row 9: (K2tog, K64, K2tog) 0 (0: 0: 0: 0: 1) times, K to end. 103 (109: 115: 121: 127: 137) sts.
Row 10: K5, P to end.
Row 11: Knit.
Row 12: MP, K until there are 5 sts on right needle, P to end.
Row 13: Knit.
Last 4 rows set the sts - front opening edge 5 sts in g st with picot worked on every 4th row and all other sts in st st.
Cont as set for a further 13 rows, ending with a WS row.
Row 27 (RS): *K2tog, rep from * to last 5 sts, K5. 54 (57: 60: 63: 66: 71) sts.
Place marker at beg of last row.
Working all side seam increases as set by back, inc 1 st at beg of 12th and foll 12th row, then on 4 foll 10th rows. 60 (63: 66: 69: 72: 77) sts.
Cont straight until left front matches back to beg of armhole shaping, ending with a WS row.
Shape raglan armhole
Cast off 5 sts at beg of next row.
55 (58: 61: 64: 67: 72) sts.
Work 3 (3: 1: 1: 1: 1) rows, end with a WS row.
Working all raglan armhole decreases as set by back, dec 1 st at raglan armhole edge of next 1 (1: 5: 5: 7: 13) rows, then on foll 14 (16: 15: 16: 17: 16) alt rows.
40 (41: 41: 43: 43: 43) sts.
Work 1 row, ending with a WS row.
Shape front neck
Next row (RS): K1, K2tog, K19 (19: 19: 21: 21: 21) and turn, leaving rem 18 (19: 19: 19: 19: 19) sts on a holder.
Dec 1 st at neck edge of next 12 rows, then on foll 0 (0: 0: 1: 1: 1) alt row **and at same time** dec 1 st at raglan armhole edge of 2nd and foll 5 (5: 5: 6: 6: 6) alt rows. 3 sts.

Work 1 row.
Next row (RS): K3tog.
Next row: P1 and fasten off.
Mark positions for 7 buttons along left front opening edge - first button to come in row 27, top button to come level with neck shaping, and rem 5 buttons evenly spaced between.

RIGHT FRONT
Work as given for left front to **.
Row 3: MP, K until there are 5 sts on right needle, (K1, yfwd, K1) into next st, (K1 wrapping yarn round needle twice) 5 times, *(K1, yfwd, K1, yfwd, K1) into next st, (K1 wrapping yarn round needle twice) 5 times, rep from * to last 2 sts, (K1, yfwd, K1) into next st, K1.
Row 4: K4, slip next 5 sts onto right needle dropping extra loops, slip same 5 sts back onto left needle and P these 5 sts tog, *K5, slip next 5 sts onto right needle dropping extra loops, slip same 5 sts back onto left needle and P these 5 sts tog, rep from * to last 8 sts, K8.
Row 5: Knit.
Row 6: P to last 5 sts, K5.
Row 7: MP, K until there are 5 sts on right needle, (K1 wrapping yarn round needle twice) 3 times, (K1, yfwd, K1, yfwd, K1) into next st, *(K1 wrapping yarn round needle twice) 5 times, (K1, yfwd, K1, yfwd, K1) into next st, rep from * to last 4 sts, (K1 wrapping yarn round needle twice) 3 times, K1.
Row 8: K1, slip next 3 sts onto right needle dropping extra loops, slip same 3 sts back onto left needle and P these 3 sts tog, K5, *slip next 5 sts onto right needle dropping extra loops, slip same 5 sts back onto left needle and P these 5 sts tog, K5, rep from * to last 8 sts, slip next 3 sts onto right needle dropping extra loops, slip same 3 sts back onto left needle and P these 3 sts tog, K5. These 8 rows complete lace border.
Row 9: K to last 0 (0: 0: 0: 0: 70) sts, (K2tog, K66, K2tog) 0 (0: 0: 0: 0: 1) times. 103 (109: 115: 121: 127: 137) sts.
Row 10: P to last 5 sts, K5.
Row 11: MP, K to end.
Row 12: P to last 5 sts, K5.
Row 13: Knit.
Last 4 rows set the sts - front opening edge 5 sts in g st with picot worked on every 4th row and all other sts in st st.
Cont as set for a further 13 rows, ending with a WS row.
Row 27 (buttonhole row) (RS): Patt 1 st, K2tog tbl, yfwd (to make a buttonhole), K2, *K2tog, rep from * to end.
54 (57: 60: 63: 66: 71) sts.

Working a further 5 buttonholes in this way to correspond with positions marked for buttons on left front and noting that no further reference will be made to buttonholes, cont as folls:
Place marker at end of last row.
Working all side seam increases as set by back, inc 1 st at end of 12th and foll 12th row, then on 4 foll 10th rows. 60 (63: 66: 69: 72: 77) sts.
Complete to match left front, reversing shapings and working first row of neck shaping as folls:
Shape front neck
Next row (RS): Patt 1 st, K2tog tbl, yfwd (to make 7th buttonhole), K until there are 18 (19: 19: 19: 19: 19) sts on right needle and slip these sts onto a holder, K to last 3 sts, K2tog tbl, K1. 21 (21: 21: 23: 23: 23) sts.

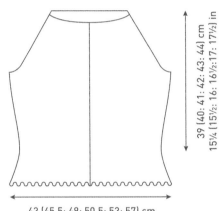

43 (45.5: 48: 50.5: 53: 57) cm
17 (18: 19: 20: 21: 22) in

39 (40: 41: 42: 43: 44) cm
15¼ (15½: 16: 16½: 17: 17½) in

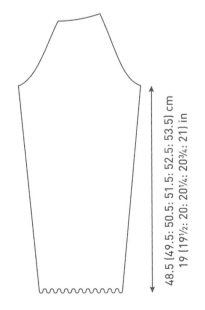

48.5 (49.5: 50.5: 51.5: 52.5: 53.5) cm
19 (19½: 20: 20¼: 20¾: 21) in

Continued on next page...

Recommendation
Suitable for the knitter with a little experience
Please see pages 6, 46 & 47 for photographs.

One size
Rowan Cocoon
2 x 100gm
Photographed in Tundra & Clay

Needles
1 pair 4½mm (no 7) (US 7) needles
1 pair 6mm (no 4) (US 10) needles

Tension
17 sts and 22 rows to 10 cm measured over
pattern using 6mm (US 10) needles.

MOON
SLOUCHY LACE PANELLED HAT

HAT
Cast on 91 sts using 4½mm (US 7) needles.
Row 1 (RS): P1, *K2, P1, rep from * to end.
Row 2: K1, *P2, K1, rep from * to end.
These 2 rows form rib.
Work in rib for a further 10 rows, ending with
a WS row.
Row 13 (RS): Rib 5, M1, (rib 9, M1) 9 times,
rib 5. 101 sts.
Row 14: Purl.
Change to 6mm (US 10) needles.
Now work in patt as folls:
Row 1 (RS): K1, *yfwd, K3, K3tog, K3, yfwd,
K1, rep from * to end.
Row 2: Purl.
Row 3: P1, *K1, yfwd, K2, K3tog, K2, yfwd, K1,
P1, rep from * to end.
Row 4: K1, *P9, K1, rep from * to end.
Row 5: P1, *K2, yfwd, K1, K3tog, K1, yfwd, K2,
P1, rep from * to end.
Row 6: As row 4.
Row 7: P1, *K3, yfwd, K3tog, yfwd, K3, P1, rep
from * to end.
Row 8: As row 4.

These 8 rows form patt.
Cont in patt for a further 24 rows, ending
with a WS row.
Shape top
Row 1 (RS): P1, *K3, K3tog, K3, P1, rep from
* to end.
81 sts.
Row 2: K1, *P7, K1, rep from * to end.
Row 3: P1, *K2, K3tog, K2, P1, rep from
* to end.
61 sts.
Row 4: K1, *P5, K1, rep from * to end.
Row 5: P1, *K1, K3tog, K1, P1, rep from
* to end.
41 sts.
Row 6: K1, *P3, K1, rep from * to end.
Row 7: P1, *K3tog, P1, rep from
* to end.
21 sts.
Row 8: K1, *P1, K1, rep from * to end.
Row 9: K1, (K2tog) 10 times.
Break yarn and thread through rem 11 sts.
Pull up tight and fasten off securely.
Join back seam.

LUNA – *Continued from previous page.*

SLEEVES (both alike)
Thread 42 (44: 46: 50: 52: 54) beads onto yarn.
Using 3¼mm (US 3) needles, work beaded
cast on as folls: *cast on 1 st, slide bead up
next to st on left needle, cast on 1 st, rep from
* until there are 84 (88: 92: 100: 104: 108)
sts on needle.
Row 1 (RS): *K2, lift 2nd st on right needle
over first st and off right needle, rep from *
to end. 42 (44: 46: 50: 52: 54) sts.
Beg with a P row and working all sleeve
increases in same way as side seam
increases, work in st st, shaping sides by
inc 1 st at each end of 18th and every foll
8th row to 64 (72: 62: 62: 70: 80) sts,
then on every foll 10th row until there
are 74 (78: 78: 82: 86: 90) sts.
Cont straight until sleeve measures 48.5
(49.5: 50.5: 51.5: 52.5: 53.5) cm, ending
with a WS row.

Shape raglan
Cast off 5 sts at beg of next 2 rows.
64 (68: 68: 72: 76: 80) sts.
Working all raglan decreases as set by raglan
armholes, dec 1 st at each end of 3rd and
5 foll 4th rows, then on every foll alt row
until 28 sts rem.
Work 1 row, ending with a WS row.
Left sleeve only
Dec 1 st at each end of next row, then cast
off 7 sts at beg of foll row. 19 sts.
Dec 1 st at beg of next row, then cast off
9 sts at beg of foll row.
Right sleeve only
Cast off 8 sts at beg and dec 1 st at end
of next row. 19 sts. Work 1 row.
Cast off 9 sts at beg and dec 1 st at end
of next row. Work 1 row.
Both sleeves
Cast off rem 9 sts.

MAKING UP
Press all pieces with a warm iron over a
damp cloth.
Join all raglan seams using back stitch
or mattress stitch if preferred.
Neckband
With RS facing and using 2¾mm (US 2)
needles, slip 18 (19: 19: 19: 19: 19) sts from
right front holder onto right needle, rejoin yarn
and pick up and knit 14 (14: 14: 16: 16: 16)
sts up right side of neck, 24 sts from top of
right sleeve, 46 (48: 48: 50: 50: 50) sts from
back, 24 sts from top of left sleeve, and 14 (14:
14: 16: 16: 16) sts down left side of neck, then
K across 18 (19: 19: 19: 19: 19) sts on left front
holder. 158 (162: 162: 168: 168: 168) sts.
Still working a picot at front opening edges on
every 4th row as set, work in g st for 6 rows,
ending with a **RS** row. Cast off knitwise (on **WS**).
Join side and sleeve seams. Sew on buttons.

RAINE
SHAWL COLLARED DOUBLE BREASTED PEPLUM CARDIGAN

Recommendation
Suitable for the knitter with a little experience
Please see pages 44 & 45 for photographs.

	XS	S	M	L	XL	XXL	
To fit	81	86	91	97	102	109	cm
bust	32	34	36	38	40	43	in

Rowan Felted Tweed
| 6 | 6 | 7 | 7 | 8 | 9 | x 50gm |

Photographed in Ancient

Needles
1 pair 3mm (no 11) (US 2/3) needles
1 pair 3¼mm (no 10) (US 3) needles
1 pair 3¾mm (no 9) (US 5) needles

Buttons – 4

Tension
23 sts and 32 rows to 10 cm measured over
stocking stitch using 3¾mm (US 5) needles.

BACK
Peplum
Cast on 24 sts using 3mm (US 2/3) needles.
Row 1 (RS): K to last 5 sts, yfwd, K2tog, K3.
Row 2: Sl 1, K4, yfwd, K2tog, K3, wrap next
st (by slipping next st on left needle onto
right needle, taking yarn to opposite side
of work between needles and then slipping
same st back onto left needle - when
working back across wrapped sts work the
wrapped st and the wrapping loop tog as
one st) and turn.
Row 3: As row 1.
Row 4: Sl 1, K4, yfwd, K2tog, K9, wrap next
st and turn.
Row 5: As row 1.
Row 6: Sl 1, K4, yfwd, K2tog, K15, wrap next
st and turn.
Row 7: K to last 5 sts, yfwd, K2tog, inc once
in each of next 3 sts.
27 sts.
Row 8: Cast off 3 sts, K until there are 5 sts
on right needle, yfwd, K2tog, K to end.
24 sts.
These 8 rows complete right side seam
shaping for back. (For left front peplum, place
marker at end of last row.)
Now work in peplum patt as folls:
Row 1 (RS): K to last 5 sts, yfwd, K2tog, K3.
Row 2: Sl 1, K4, yfwd, K2tog, K to end.
Rows 3 and 4: As rows 1 and 2.
Row 5: K to last 5 sts, yfwd, K2tog, inc once
in each of next 3 sts. 27 sts.
Row 6: Cast off 3 sts, K until there are 5 sts
on right needle, yfwd, K2tog, K to end.
24 sts.
Last 6 rows form peplum patt.**
Rep these 6 rows a further 25 (26: 28: 30:
32: 35) times more, then work row 1 again.
***Now shape left side seam for back as folls:
Row 1 (WS): Sl 1, K4, yfwd, K2tog, K15,
wrap next st and turn.
Row 2: K to last 5 sts, yfwd, K2tog, K3.
Row 3: Sl 1, K4, yfwd, K2tog, K9, wrap next
st and turn.
Row 4: As row 2.
Row 5: Sl 1, K4, yfwd, K2tog, K3, wrap next
st and turn.
Row 6: As row 2.
Cast off (on **WS**).***

Upper back
With RS of peplum facing and using 3¾mm
(US 5) needles, pick up and knit 77 (83: 89:
95: 101: 111) sts evenly along shorter row-
end edge of peplum.
Beg with a **purl** row, now work in st st
throughout as folls:
Work 5 rows, ending with a WS row.
Next row (inc) (RS): K3, M1, K to last 3 sts,
M1, K3.
Working all side seam increases as set by last
row, inc 1 st at each end of 6th and 4 (6: 6: 8:
8: 9) foll 6th rows, then on 5 (3: 3: 1: 1: 0) foll
4th rows.
99 (105: 111: 117: 123: 133) sts.
Work 7 rows, ending with a WS row. (Back
should measure 20 (21: 21: 22: 22: 23) cm
from peplum pick-up row.)
Shape armholes
Cast off 4 (5: 5: 6: 6: 7) sts at beg of next
2 rows.
91 (95: 101: 105: 111: 119) sts.
Dec 1 st at each end of next 5 (5: 7: 7: 9: 9)
rows, then on foll 3 (4: 4: 5: 5: 7) alt rows,
then on foll 4th row.
73 (75: 77: 79: 81: 85) sts.
Cont straight until armhole measures 19 (19:
20: 20: 21: 21) cm, ending with a WS row.
Shape back neck and shoulders
Cast off 7 (7: 7: 7: 7: 8) sts at beg of next
2 rows.
59 (61: 63: 65: 67: 69) sts.
Next row (RS): Cast off 7 (7: 7: 7: 7: 8) sts,
K until there are 10 (10: 11: 11: 12: 12) sts
on right needle and turn, leaving rem sts on
a holder.
Work each side of neck separately.
Cast off 4 sts at beg of next row.
Cast off rem 6 (6: 7: 7: 8: 8) sts.
With RS facing, rejoin yarn to rem sts, cast off
centre 25 (27: 27: 29: 29: 29) sts, K to end.
Complete to match first side, reversing
shapings.

LEFT FRONT
Peplum
Work as given for back peplum to **, noting
the bracketed exception.
Rep last 6 rows a further 7 (7: 8: 9: 10: 12)
times more, then patt rows 1 to 4 again.

Now shape front curve as folls:
Next row (RS): K to last 8 sts, K2tog, patt to end.
Working all decreases as set by last row and keeping patt correct, dec 1 st at end of 4th and 4 foll 4th rows, then on every foll alt row until 9 sts rem, ending with a **RS** row.
Next row (WS): Patt to last 2 sts, K2tog.
Keeping patt correct as far as possible and then completing peplum in g st, dec 1 st at beg of next row and at same edge on every foll row until 1 st remains.
Fasten off and break yarn.

Upper left front
With RS of peplum facing and using 3¾mm (US 5) needles, pick up and knit 53 (56: 59: 62: 65: 70) sts evenly along shorter row-end edge of peplum, between cast-on edge and fasten-off point.
Now work in patt as folls:
Row 1 (WS): K4, (P1, K1) 9 times, P1, K4, P to end.
Row 2: K to last 23 sts, (K1, P1) 9 times, K5.
Row 3: Cast on 1 st, cast off 1 st (to make picot), K until there are 4 sts on right needle, (K1, P1) 9 times, K5, P to end.
Row 4: K to last 23 sts, (P1, K1) 9 times, P1, K4.
These 4 rows set the sts - front opening edge sts in double moss st with g st each side, picots along front opening edge on every 4th row and rem sts in st st.
Keeping sts correct as now set and working all side seam increases as set by back, inc 1 st at beg of 2nd and 2 foll 6th rows.
56 (59: 62: 65: 68: 73) sts.
Work 5 rows, ending with a WS row.
Shape front slope
Next row (RS): K3, M1 (for side seam inc), K to last 29 sts, K2tog tbl (for front slope dec), patt to end.
56 (59: 62: 65: 68: 73) sts.
Working all front slope decreases as set by last row, cont as folls:
Inc 1 st at side seam edge of 6th and 1 (3: 3: 5: 5: 6) foll 6th rows, then on 5 (3: 3: 1: 1: 0) foll 4th rows **and at same time** dec 1 st at front slope edge on 26th (20th: 20th: 18th: 20th: 20th) and foll 0 (0: 0: 18th: 20th: 20th) row. 62 (65: 68: 70: 73: 78) sts.
Work 7 rows, dec 0 (1: 1: 0: 0: 0) st at front slope edge of 4th of these rows and ending with a WS row.
62 (64: 67: 70: 73: 78) sts.

Shape armhole
Keeping patt correct, cast off 4 (5: 5: 6: 6: 7) sts at beg of next row.
58 (59: 62: 64: 67: 71) sts.
Work 1 row.
Dec 1 st at armhole edge of next 5 (5: 7: 7: 9: 9) rows, then on foll 3 (4: 4: 5: 5: 7) alt rows, then on foll 4th row **and at same time** dec 1 st at front slope edge of 11th (15th: 15th: 5th: 11th: 9th) row.
48 (48: 49: 50: 51: 53) sts.
Dec 1 st at front slope edge only on 22nd (18th: 16th: 2nd: 8th: 2nd) and foll 0 (0: 0: 18th: 20th: 20th) row.
47 (47: 48: 48: 49: 51) sts.
Cont straight until left front matches back to beg of shoulder shaping, ending with a WS row.
Shape shoulder
Keeping patt correct, cast off 7 (7: 7: 7: 7: 8) sts at beg of next and foll alt row, then 6 (6: 7: 7: 8: 8) sts at beg of foll alt row. 27 sts.
Cont in patt on these 27 sts only (for back collar extension) for a further 6.5 (7: 7: 7.5: 7.5: 7.5) cm, ending at outer edge.
Next row: Patt 21 sts, wrap next st and turn.
Next row: Patt to end.
Next row: Patt 15 sts, wrap next st and turn.
Next row: Patt to end.
Next row: Patt 9 sts, wrap next st and turn.
Next row: Patt to end.
Cast off all 27 sts in patt.

RIGHT FRONT
Peplum
Cast on 1 st using 3mm (US 2/3) needles.
Now shape front curve as folls:
Row 1 (RS): Inc in st. 2 sts.
Row 2: K1, inc in next st. 3 sts.
Row 3: Inc in first st, K2. 4 sts.
Row 4: K3, inc in last st. 5 sts.
Row 5: Inc in first st, K4. 6 sts.
Row 6: K5, inc in last st. 7 sts.
Row 7: Inc in first st, K1, yfwd, K2tog, K3. 8 sts.
Row 8: K5, inc in next st, K2. 9 sts.
Row 9: K2, inc in next st, K1, yfwd, K2tog, inc once in each of next 3 sts.
Row 10: Cast off 3 sts (one st on right needle), K4, inc in next st, K4. 11 sts.
Row 11: K to last 7 sts, inc in next st, K1, yfwd, K2tog, K3. 12 sts.
Row 12: K5, yfwd, K2tog, K to end.
Keeping patt correct as now set and as given for back and left front peplums, cont in patt, inc 1 st (as set by row 11) on next and every foll alt row to 19 sts, then on every foll 4th row until there are 24 sts.

Cont straight in patt until straight row-end edge of this peplum measures same as straight row-end edge of left front peplum from marker to fasten-off point, ending with a RS row.
Complete as given for back peplum from *** to ***.
Upper right front
With RS of peplum facing and using 3¾mm (US 5) needles, pick up and knit 53 (56: 59: 62: 65: 70) sts evenly along shorter row-end edge of peplum, between cast-on and cast-off edges.
Now work in patt as folls:
Row 1 (WS): P to last 27 sts, K4, (P1, K1) 9 times, P1, K4.
Row 2: Cast on 1 st, cast off 1 st (to make picot), K until there are 3 sts on right needle, K2tog tbl, (yfwd) twice, K2tog (to make a buttonhole - work into back and front of double yfwd on next row), (P1, K1) 6 times, P1, K2tog tbl, (yfwd) twice, K2tog (to make a buttonhole - work into back and front of double yfwd on next row), K to end. (First pair of buttonholes completed.)
Row 3: P to last 27 sts, K4, (K1, P1) 9 times, K5.
Row 4: K4, (P1, K1) 9 times, P1, K to end.
Row 5: P to last 27 sts, K4, (P1, K1) 9 times, P1, K4.
Row 6: Cast on 1 st, cast off 1 st (to make picot), K until there are 4 sts on right needle, (K1, P1) 9 times, K to last 3 sts, M1, K3.
Last 4 rows set the sts - front opening edge sts in double moss st with g st each side, picots along front opening edge on every 4th row and rem sts in st st.
Keeping sts correct as now set and working all side seam increases as set by back, inc 1 st at end of 6th and foll 6th row.
56 (59: 62: 65: 68: 73) sts.
Work 1 row.
Row 20 (RS): K3, K2tog tbl, (yfwd) twice, K2tog (to make a buttonhole - work into back and front of double yfwd on next row), patt 13 sts, K2tog tbl, (yfwd) twice, K2tog (to make a buttonhole - work into back and front of double yfwd on next row), K to end. (Second pair of buttonholes completed.)
Work 3 rows, ending with a WS row.
Shape front slope
Next row (RS): Patt 27 sts, K2tog (for front slope dec), K to last 3 sts, M1 (for side seam inc), K3. 56 (59: 62: 65: 68: 73) sts.
Working all front slope decreases as set by last row, complete to match left front, reversing shapings.

SLEEVES (both alike)

Cast on 47 (47: 49: 51: 51: 53) sts using 3¼mm (US 3) needles.

Row 1 (RS): K1, *P1, K1, rep from * to end.

Row 2: As row 1.

Rows 3 and 4: P1, *K1, P1, rep from * to end.

These 4 rows form double moss st.

Cont in double moss st for a further 26 rows, inc 1 st at each end of 11th of these rows and foll 10th row, taking inc sts into patt and ending with a WS row.

51 (51: 53: 55: 55: 57) sts.

Change to 3¾mm (US 5) needles.

Beg with a K row and working all sleeve increases in same way as side seam increases, now work in st st, shaping sides by inc 1 st at each end of 5th and every foll 10th row to 55 (63: 61: 61: 69: 69) sts, then on every foll 12th row until there are 69 (71: 73: 75: 77: 79) sts.

Cont straight until sleeve measures 44 (45: 46: 47: 48: 49) cm, ending with a WS row.

Shape top

Cast off 4 (5: 5: 6: 6: 7) sts at beg of next 2 rows.

61 (61: 63: 63: 65: 65) sts.

Dec 1 st at each end of next 3 rows, then on foll alt row, then on 6 foll 4th rows.

41 (41: 43: 43: 45: 45) sts.

Work 1 row, ending with a WS row.

Dec 1 st at each end of next and every foll alt row to 33 sts, then on foll 5 rows, ending with a WS row.

Cast off rem 23 sts.

MAKING UP

Press all pieces with a warm iron over a damp cloth.

Join both shoulder seams using back stitch or mattress stitch if preferred.

Join cast-off ends of back collar extensions, then sew one edge to back neck.

Join side seams. Join sleeve seams. Sew sleeves into armholes. Sew on buttons.

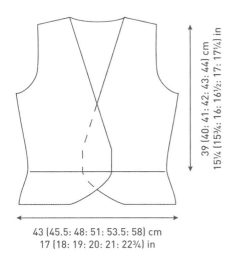

43 (45.5: 48: 51: 53.5: 58) cm
17 (18: 19: 20: 21: 22¾) in

39 (40: 41: 42: 43: 44) cm
15¼ (15¾: 16: 16½: 17: 17¼) in

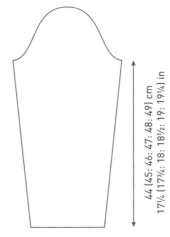

44 (45: 46: 47: 48: 49) cm
17¼ (17¾: 18: 18½: 19: 19¼) in

FAYER

RELAXED SWEATER WITH GENEROUS NECK

Recommendation

Suitable for the novice knitter

Please see pages 48 & 49 for photographs.

	XS	S	M	L	XL	XXL	
To fit	81	86	91	97	102	109	cm
bust	32	34	36	38	40	43	in

Rowan Alpaca Cotton

| | 7 | 7 | 8 | 8 | 9 | 9 | x 50gm |

Photographed in Rice

Needles

1 pair 5mm (no 6) (US 8) needles
1 pair 5½mm (no 5) (US 9) needles
1 pair 6mm (no 4) (US 10) needles

Tension

16 sts and 22 rows to 10 cm measured over
stocking stitch using 5½mm (US 9) needles.

BACK

Cast on 73 (77: 81: 85: 89: 95) sts using
5mm (US 8) needles.
Beg with a K row, work in st st for 10 rows,
ending with a WS row.
Change to 5½mm (US 9) needles.
Work in st st for a further 22 rows, ending with
a WS row.
Next row (dec) (RS): K3, K2tog, K to last 5 sts,
K2tog tbl, K3.
Working all side seam decreases as set by last
row, dec 1 st at each end of 12th and 2 foll
8th rows.
65 (69: 73: 77: 81: 87) sts.
Cont straight until back measures 41 (41: 42:
42: 42: 42) cm, ending with a WS row.
Next row (inc) (RS): K3, M1, K to last 3 sts,
M1, K3.
Working all side seam increases as set by last
row, inc 1 st at each end of 18th row.
69 (73: 77: 81: 85: 91) sts.
Cont straight until back measures 53 (53: 54:
54: 54: 54) cm, ending with a WS row.

Shape armholes

Cast off 2 (3: 3: 4: 4: 5) sts at beg of next
2 rows. 65 (67: 71: 73: 77: 81) sts.
Dec 1 st at each end of next 3 (3: 5: 5: 5: 7)
rows, then on foll 3 (3: 2: 2: 3: 2) alt rows,
then on foll 4th row.
51 (53: 55: 57: 59: 61) sts.
Cont straight until armhole measures
18 (19: 19: 20: 21: 22) cm, ending with
a WS row.

Shape back neck and shoulders

Next row (RS): Cast off 3 (4: 4: 4: 5: 5) sts,
K until there are 8 (8: 9: 9: 9: 10) sts on right
needle and turn, leaving rem sts on a holder.
Work each side of neck separately.
Cast off 4 sts at beg of next row.
Cast off rem 4 (4: 5: 5: 5: 6) sts.
With RS facing, rejoin yarn to rem sts, cast off
centre 29 (29: 29: 31: 31: 31) sts, K to end.
Complete to match first side, reversing
shapings.

FRONT

Work as given for back until 12 (12: 12: 14:
14: 14) rows less have been worked than on
back to beg of shoulder shaping, ending with
a WS row.

Shape front neck

Next row (RS): K13 (14: 15: 16: 17: 18)
and turn, leaving rem sts on a holder.
Work each side of neck separately.
Dec 1 st at neck edge of next 4 rows, then
on foll 2 (2: 2: 3: 3: 3) alt rows.
7 (8: 9: 9: 10: 11) sts.
Work 3 rows, ending with a WS row.

Shape shoulder

Cast off 3 (4: 4: 4: 5: 5) sts at beg of next row.
Work 1 row.
Cast off rem 4 (4: 5: 5: 5: 6) sts.
With RS facing, rejoin yarn to rem sts, cast off
centre 25 sts, K to end.
Complete to match first side, reversing
shapings.

SLEEVES (both alike)

Cast on 43 (45: 45: 47: 49: 51) sts using
6mm (US 10) needles.
Beg with a K row, work in st st for 18 (20:
20: 20: 22: 24) rows, ending with a WS
row.
Change to 5½mm (US 9) needles.
Beg with a K row and working all sleeve
increases in same way as side seam increases,
now work in st st, shaping sides by inc 1 st at
each end of 31st and foll 40th row.
47 (49: 49: 51: 53: 55) sts.
Cont straight until sleeve measures 52 (54:
55: 56: 58: 60) cm, ending with a WS row.

Shape top

Cast off 2 (3: 3: 4: 4: 5) sts at beg of next
2 rows.
43 (43: 43: 43: 45: 45) sts.
Dec 1 st at each end of next 3 rows, then
on foll alt row, then on 3 (4: 4: 5: 4: 5) foll
4th rows.
29 (27: 27: 25: 29: 27) sts.
Work 1 row, ending with a WS row.
Dec 1 st at each end of next and foll 2 (1: 1:
0: 2: 1) alt rows, then on foll 3 rows, ending
with a WS row.
Cast off rem 17 sts.

MAKING UP

Press all pieces with a warm iron over a damp
cloth.
Join right shoulder seam using back stitch or
mattress stitch if preferred.

Collar

With RS facing and using 5mm (US 8) needles, pick up and knit 14 (14: 14: 16: 16: 16) sts down left side of neck, 25 sts from front, 14 (14: 14: 16: 16: 16) sts up right side of neck, then 38 (38: 38: 40: 40: 40) sts from back. 91 (91: 91: 97: 97: 97) sts.

Beg with a K row (to reverse RS of work for collar), work in st st for 16 rows, ending with a WS row.

Change to 5½mm (US 9) needles.

Row 17 (RS of collar, WS of body): K2, *M1, K3, rep from * to last 2 sts, M1, K2. 121 (121: 121: 129: 129: 129) sts.

Cont in st st for a further 19 rows, ending with a WS row.

Change to 6mm (US 10) needles.

Work a further 16 rows, ending with a WS row. Cast off loosely.

Join left shoulder and collar seam, reversing seam for collar. Join side seams. Join sleeve seams, reversing seams for first 18 (20: 20: 20: 22: 24) rows. Sew sleeves into armholes. Fold 7 (8: 8: 8: 9: 10) cm cuff to RS.

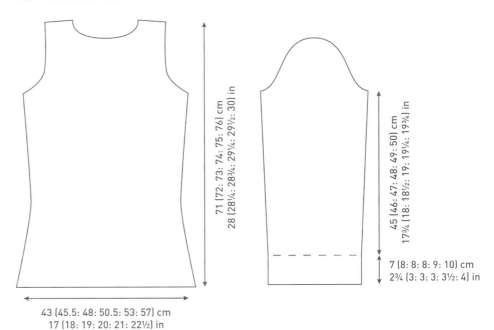

71 (72: 73: 74: 75: 76) cm
28 (28¼: 28¾: 29¼: 29½: 30) in

43 (45.5: 48: 50.5: 53: 57) cm
17 (18: 19: 20: 21: 22½) in

45 (46: 47: 48: 49: 50) cm
17¾ (18: 18½: 19: 19¼: 19¾) in

7 (8: 8: 8: 9: 10) cm
2¾ (3: 3: 3: 3½: 4) in

Recommendation
Suitable for the novice
Please see pages 50 & 53 for photographs.

Rowan Alpaca Cotton
4   x 50gm
Photographed in Rice

Crochet hook
7.00mm (no 2) (US K10½) crochet hook

Tension
3 pattern repeats (15 sts) and 6 rows to 10
cm measured over pattern using 7.00mm (US
K10½) crochet hook.

Finished size
Completed scarf measures 193 cm (76 ins)
long and is 35 cm (14 ins) wide.

Crochet abbreviations
ch = chain; **ss** = slip stitch; **dc** = double
crochet; **tr** = treble; **sp** = space.

CLARITY
COSY LACY CROCHET SCARF

SCARF
First section
Using 7.00mm (US K10½) crochet hook make
49 ch.
Row 1 (RS): Miss 5 ch, *(2 tr, 1 ch and 2 tr)
into next ch**, miss 4 ch, rep from * to end,
ending last rep at **, miss 2 ch, 1 tr into last
ch, turn.
9 patt reps.
***Row 2:** 3 ch (counts as first tr), miss tr at
base of 3 ch and next 2 tr, *(2 tr, 1 ch and 2 tr)
into next ch sp**, miss 4 tr, rep from * to end,
ending last rep at **, miss 2 tr, 1 tr into top
of 3 ch at beg of previous row, turn.
Row 2 forms patt.
Cont in patt for a further 27 rows, ending with
a RS row.
Now shape end as folls:
Row 1 (WS): 3 ch (counts as first tr), miss tr at
base of 3 ch and next 2 tr, (1 tr, 1 ch and
2 tr) into first ch sp, *miss 4 tr**, (2 tr, 1 ch
and 2 tr) into next ch sp, rep from * to end,
ending last rep at **, (2 tr, 1 ch and 1 tr) into
last ch sp, miss 2 tr, 1 tr into top of 3 ch at
beg of previous row, turn.
Row 2: 3 ch (counts as first tr), miss tr at
base of 3 ch and next tr, (1 tr, 1 ch and 2 tr)
into first ch sp, *miss 4 tr**, (2 tr, 1 ch and
2 tr) into next ch sp, rep from * to end, ending
last rep at **, (2 tr, 1 ch and 1 tr) into last ch
sp, miss 1 tr, 1 tr into top of 3 ch at beg of
previous row, turn.
Row 3: 4 ch (counts as first tr and 1 ch), miss
tr at base of 3 ch and next tr, 2 tr into first ch
sp, *miss 4 tr**, (2 tr, 1 ch and 2 tr) into next
ch sp, rep from * to end, ending last rep at **,
2 tr into last ch sp, 1 ch, miss 1 tr, 1 tr into
top of 3 ch at beg of previous row, turn.

Row 4: 4 ch (counts as first tr and 1 ch),
miss tr at base of 3 ch, 2 tr into first ch sp,
*miss 4 tr**, (2 tr, 1 ch and 2 tr) into next ch
sp, rep from * to end, ending last rep at **,
2 tr into last ch sp, 1 ch, 1 tr into 3rd of 4 ch
at beg of previous row, turn.
Row 5: 3 ch (counts as first tr), miss tr at
base of 3 ch, 2 tr into first ch sp, *miss 4 tr**,
(2 tr, 1 ch and 2 tr) into next ch sp, rep from
* to end, ending last rep at **, 2 tr into last
ch sp, 1 tr into 3rd of 4 ch at beg of previous
row, turn.
Row 6: 3 ch (counts as first tr), 1 tr into tr
at base of 3 ch, *miss 4 tr**, (2 tr, 1 ch and
2 tr) into next ch sp, rep from * to end,
ending last rep at **, 2 tr into top of 3 ch
at beg of previous row, turn.
Row 7: 3 ch (counts as first tr), miss tr at
base of 3 ch and next 3 tr, *(2 tr, 1 ch and
2 tr) into next ch sp**, miss 4 tr, rep from *
to end, ending last rep at **, miss 3 tr, 1 tr
into top of 3 ch at beg of previous row, turn.
Row 8: 3 ch (counts as first tr), miss tr at
base of 3 ch and next 2 tr, *(2 tr, 1 ch and 2 tr)
into next ch sp**, miss 4 tr, rep from * to end,
ending last rep at **, miss 2 tr, 1 tr into top of
3 ch at beg of previous row, turn. 7 patt reps.
Rows 9 to 16: As rows 1 to 8. 5 patt reps.
Rows 17 to 23: As rows 1 to 7. 3 patt reps.
Row 24: 3 ch (counts as first tr), miss tr at
base of 3 ch and next 2 tr, (1 tr, 1 ch and 2 tr)
into first ch sp, miss 4 tr, (2 tr, 1 ch and 2 tr)
into next ch sp, miss 4 tr, (2 tr, 1 ch and 1 tr)
into last ch sp, miss 2 tr, 1 tr into top of 3 ch
at beg of previous row, turn.
Row 25: 4 ch (counts as first tr and 1 ch),
miss tr at base of 3 ch and next tr, 2 tr into
first ch sp, miss 4 tr, (2 tr, 1 ch and 2 tr) into

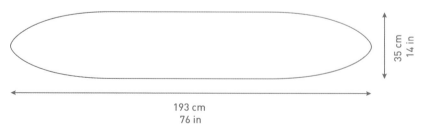

193 cm
76 in

35 cm
14 in

Continued on next page...

GOODWILL

TWEED JACKET WITH COVERED BUTTONS & CROCHET TRIMS

Recommendation
Suitable for the knitter with a little experience
Please see pages 54, 55 & 56 for photographs.

	XS	S	M	L	XL	XXL	
To fit	81	86	91	97	102	109	cm
bust	32	34	36	38	40	43	in

Rowan Felted Tweed Aran
	10	11	11	12	12	13	x 50gm

Photographed in Pebble

Needles
1 pair 5mm (no 6) (US 8) needles
4.00mm (no 8) (US G6) crochet hook

Extras – 5 button frames

Tension
18 sts and 25 rows to 10 cm measured over
pattern using 5mm (US 8) needles.

Crochet abbreviations
ch = chain; **dc** = double crochet.

BACK
Cast on 71 (75: 79: 85: 89: 95) sts using
5mm (US 8) needles.
Row 1 (RS): K0 (0: 0: 1: 1: 0), *P1, K1, rep
from * to last 1 (1: 1: 0: 0: 1) st, P (1: 1: 0: 0: 1).
Row 2: As row 1.
Now work in patt as folls:
Rows 1 and 2: P0 (0: 0: 1: 1: 0), *K1, P1, rep
from * to last 1 (1: 1: 0: 0: 1) st, K (1: 1: 0: 0: 1).
Rows 3 and 4: K0 (0: 0: 1: 1: 0), *P1, K1, rep
from * to last 1 (1: 1: 0: 0: 1) st, P (1: 1: 0: 0: 1).
Rows 5 to 12: As rows 1 to 4, twice.
Row 13: Purl.
Row 14: Knit.
These 14 rows form patt - 12 rows in double
moss st followed by 2 rows in rev st st.
Place markers at both ends of last row to
denote top of side seam openings.
Cont in patt, dec 1 st at each end of next and
2 foll 6th rows. 65 (69: 73: 79: 83: 89) sts.
Work 17 rows, ending with a WS row.
Inc 1 st at each end of next and 4 foll 8th
rows, taking inc sts into patt.
75 (79: 83: 89: 93: 99) sts.
Work 9 (9: 11: 11: 11: 11) rows, ending after
patt row 2 (2: 4: 4: 4: 4) and with a WS row.
(Back should meas 35 (35: 36: 36: 36: 36) cm.)

Shape armholes
Keeping patt correct, cast off 3 (4: 4: 5: 5: 6) sts
at beg of next 2 rows. 69 (71: 75: 79: 83: 87) sts.
Dec 1 st at each end of next 3 (3: 5: 5: 7: 7)
rows, then on foll 3 (3: 2: 3: 2: 3) alt rows,
then on foll 4th row.
55 (57: 59: 61: 63: 65) sts.
Cont straight until armhole measures 18 (19:
19: 20: 21: 22) cm, ending with a WS row.
Shape back neck and shoulders
Cast off 5 (5: 5: 5: 6: 6) sts at beg of next
2 rows.
45 (47: 49: 51: 51: 53) sts.
Next row (RS): Cast off 5 (5: 5: 5: 6: 6) sts,
patt until there are 8 (8: 9: 9: 8: 9) sts on right
needle and turn, leaving rem sts on a holder.
Work each side of neck separately.
Cast off 3 sts at beg of next row.
Cast off rem 5 (5: 6: 6: 5: 6) sts.
With RS facing, rejoin yarn to rem sts, cast off
centre 19 (21: 21: 23: 23: 23) sts, patt to end.
Complete to match first side, reversing
shapings.

POCKET LININGS (make 2)
Cast on 17 (17: 19: 19: 21: 21) sts using
5mm (US 8) needles.
Beg with a P row, work 24 rows in rev st st,
ending with a WS row.
Break yarn and leave sts on a holder.

Continued on next page...

---

next ch sp, miss 4 tr, 2 tr into last ch sp, 1
ch, miss 1 tr, 1 tr into top of 3 ch at beg of
previous row, turn.
Row 26: 3 ch (counts as first tr), miss tr at
base of 3 ch, 2 tr into first ch sp, miss 4 tr,
(2 tr, 1 ch and 2 tr) into next ch sp, miss 4 tr,
2 tr into last ch sp, 1 tr into 3rd of 4 ch at
beg of previous row, turn.
Row 27: 3 ch (counts as first tr), 1 tr into tr
at base of 3 ch, miss 4 tr, (2 tr, 1 ch and 2 tr)
into next ch sp, miss 4 tr, 2 tr into top of 3 ch
at beg of previous row, turn.
Row 28: 3 ch (counts as first tr), miss tr at
base of 3 ch and next 3 tr, (2 tr, 1 ch and 2 tr)

into next ch sp, miss 3 tr, 1 tr into top of 3 ch
at beg of previous row, turn. 1 patt rep.
Fasten off.
Second section
With RS facing and using 7.00mm (US K10½)
crochet hook, return to foundation ch edge of
first section and attach yarn at base of tr at
end of row 1 of first section.
Working into foundation ch edge of first
section, cont as folls:
Row 1 (RS): 3 ch (counts as first tr), miss ch
at base of these 3 ch and next 2 ch, *(2 tr, 1
ch and 2 tr) into next ch**, miss 4 ch, rep from
* to end, ending last rep at **, miss 2 ch, 1 tr

into last ch, turn. 9 patt reps.
Now complete as given for first section from
***.

EDGING
With RS facing and using 7.00mm (US
K10½) crochet hook, attach yarn to one end
of foundation ch at centre of scarf, now work
around entire outer edge of both sections as
folls: 1 ch (does NOT count as st), 1 dc into
place where yarn was rejoined, *5 tr into next
row-end, 1 dc into next row-end, rep from * to
end, replacing dc at end of last rep with ss to
first dc. Fasten off.

LEFT FRONT

Cast on 42 (44: 46: 49: 51: 54) sts using 5mm (US 8) needles.

Row 1 (RS): K0 (0: 0: 1: 1: 0), *P1, K1, rep from * to end.

Row 2: K1, *P1, K1, rep from * to last 1 (1: 1: 0: 0: 1) st, P1 (1: 1: 0: 0: 1).

Now work in patt as folls:

Rows 1 (RS): P0 (0: 0: 1: 1: 0), *K1, P1, rep from * to end.

Row 2: P1, *K1, P1, rep from * to last 1 (1: 1: 0: 0: 1) st, K1 (1: 1: 0: 0: 1).

Row 3: K0 (0: 0: 1: 1: 0), *P1, K1, rep from * to end.

Row 4: K1, *P1, K1, rep from * to last 1 (1: 1: 0: 0: 1) st, P1 (1: 1: 0: 0: 1).

Rows 5 to 12: As rows 1 to 4, twice.

Row 13: Purl.

Row 14: Knit.

These 14 rows form patt - 12 rows in double moss st followed by 2 rows in rev st st.

Place marker at end of last row to denote top of side seam opening.

Cont in patt, dec 1 st at beg of next and 2 foll 6th rows, ending after patt row 13 and with a **RS** row. 39 (41: 43: 46: 48: 51) sts.

Place pocket

Next row (WS): K16, cast off next 17 (17: 19: 19: 21: 21) sts knitwise, K to end.

Next row: Patt 6 (8: 8: 11: 11: 14) sts, with RS facing patt across 17 (17: 19: 19: 21: 21) sts of first pocket lining, patt to end.

Work 15 rows, ending with a WS row.

Inc 1 st at beg of next and 4 foll 8th rows, taking inc sts into patt.

44 (46: 48: 51: 53: 56) sts.

Work 9 (9: 11: 11: 11: 11) rows, ending with a WS row.

Shape armhole

Keeping patt correct, cast off 3 (4: 4: 5: 5: 6) sts at beg of next row. 41 (42: 44: 46: 48: 50) sts.

Work 1 row.

Dec 1 st at armhole edge of next 3 (3: 5: 5: 7: 7) rows, then on foll 3 (3: 2: 3: 2: 3) alt rows, then on foll 4th row. 34 (35: 36: 37: 38: 39) sts.

Cont straight until 11 (11: 11: 13: 13: 13) rows less have been worked than on back to beg of shoulder shaping, ending with a **RS** row.

Shape front neck

Keeping patt correct, cast off 13 (14: 14: 14: 14: 14) sts at beg of next row. 21 (21: 22: 23: 24: 25) sts.

Dec 1 st at neck edge of next 4 rows, then on foll 2 (2: 2: 3: 3: 3) alt rows. 15 (15: 16: 16: 17: 18) sts.

Work 2 rows, ending with a WS row.

Shape shoulder

Cast off 5 (5: 5: 5: 6: 6) sts at beg of next and foll alt row.

Work 1 row.

Cast off rem 5 (5: 6: 6: 5: 6) sts.

Mark positions for 5 buttons along left front opening edge - first to come in row 9, last to come 2 cm below neck shaping, and rem 3 buttons evenly spaced between.

RIGHT FRONT

Cast on 42 (44: 46: 49: 51: 54) sts using 5mm (US 8) needles.

Row 1 (RS): K1, *P1, K1, rep from * to last 1 (1: 1: 0: 0: 1) st, P1 (1: 1: 0: 0: 1).

Row 2: K0 (0: 0: 1: 1: 0), *P1, K1, rep from * to end.

Now work in patt as folls:

Rows 1 (RS): P1, *K1, P1, rep from * to last 1 (1: 1: 0: 0: 1) st, K1 (1: 1: 0: 0: 1).

Row 2: P0 (0: 0: 1: 1: 0), *K1, P1, rep from * to end.

Row 3: K1, *P1, K1, rep from * to last 1 (1: 1: 0: 0: 1) st, P1 (1: 1: 0: 0: 1).

Row 4: K0 (0: 0: 1: 1: 0), *P1, K1, rep from * to end.

Rows 5 and 6: As rows 1 and 2.

Row 7 (buttonhole row) (RS): K1, P1, K1, P2tog tbl, yrn (to make a buttonhole), *P1, K1, rep from * to last 1 (1: 1: 0: 0: 1) st, P1 (1: 1: 0: 0: 1).

Row 8: As row 4.

Rows 9 to 12: As rows 1 to 4.

Row 13: Purl.

Row 14: Knit.

These 14 rows form patt and place first buttonhole.

Working a further 4 buttonholes as set by patt row 7 to correspond with positions marked on left front for buttons and noting that no further reference will be made to buttonholes, cont as folls:

Place marker at beg of last row to denote top of side seam opening.

Cont in patt, dec 1 st at end of next and 2 foll 6th rows, ending after patt row 13 and with a **RS** row.

39 (41: 43: 46: 48: 51) sts.

Place pocket

Next row (WS): K6 (8: 8: 11: 11: 14), cast off next 17 (17: 19: 19: 21: 21) sts knitwise, K to end.

Next row: Patt 16 sts, with RS facing patt across 17 (17: 19: 19: 21: 21) sts of first pocket lining, patt to end.

Complete to match left front, reversing shapings.

SLEEVES (both alike)

First section

Cast on 21 (22: 23: 24: 25: 26) sts using 5mm (US 2/3) needles.

Row 1 (RS): *K1, P1, rep from * to last 1 (0: 1: 0: 1: 0) st, K1 (0: 1: 0: 1: 0).

Row 2: K1 (0: 1: 0: 1: 0), *P1, K1, rep from * to end.

Row 3: *P1, K1, rep from * to last 1 (0: 1: 0: 1: 0) st, P1 (0: 1: 0: 1: 0).

Row 4: P1 (0: 1: 0: 1: 0), *K1, P1, rep from * to end.

These 4 rows form double moss st.

Work in double moss st for a further 10 rows, ending with a WS row.

Break yarn and leave sts on a holder.

53 (54: 55: 56: 57: 58) cm
21 (21¼: 21¾: 22: 22½: 23) in

41.5 (44: 46: 49: 51.5: 55) cm
16 (17¼: 18: 19¼: 20: 21½) in

37 (38: 39: 40: 41: 42) cm
14½ (15: 15¼: 15¾: 16: 16½) in

Second section

Cast on 21 (22: 23: 24: 25: 26) sts using 5mm (US 2/3) needles.

Row 1 (RS): K1 (0: 1: 0: 1: 0), *P1, K1, rep from * to end.

Row 2: *K1, P1, rep from * to last 1 (0: 1: 0: 1: 0) st, K1 (0: 1: 0: 1: 0).

Row 3: P1 (0: 1: 0: 1: 0), *K1, P1, rep from * to end.

Row 4: *P1, K1, rep from * to last 1 (0: 1: 0: 1: 0) st, P1 (0: 1: 0: 1: 0).

These 4 rows form double moss st.
Work in double moss st for a further 10 rows, ending with a WS row.

Join sections

Next row (RS): Patt to last st of second section, inc in last st, then patt across sts of first section. 43 (45: 47: 49: 51: 53) sts.

Working a further 5 (7: 7: 9: 11: 13) rows in double moss st and then 2 rows in rev st st, now work in patt as given for back, shaping sides by inc 1 st at each end of 2nd and 4 foll 16th (16th: 16th: 16th: 18th: 18th) rows, taking inc sts into patt.
53 (55: 57: 59: 61: 63) sts.

Cont straight until sleeve measures approx 37 (38: 39: 40: 41: 42) cm, ending after patt row 2 (2: 4: 4: 4: 4) and with a WS row.

Shape top

Keeping patt correct, cast off 3 (4: 4: 5: 5: 6) sts at beg of next 2 rows. 47 (47: 49: 49: 51: 51) sts.
Dec 1 st at each end of next 3 rows, then on foll alt row, then on 4 (5: 4: 5: 5: 6) foll 4th rows. 31 (29: 33: 31: 33: 31) sts.
Work 1 row, ending with a WS row.
Dec 1 st at each end of next and foll 3 (2: 4: 3: 4: 3) alt rows, then on foll 3 rows, ending with a WS row.
Cast off rem 17 sts.

MAKING UP

Press all pieces with a warm iron over a damp cloth.
Join both shoulder seams using back stitch or mattress stitch if preferred.

Lower back edging

With RS facing and using 4.00mm (US G6) crochet hook, attach yarn to left side seam edge of back at marker, 1 ch (does NOT count as st), now work 1 row of dc down left back side opening edge, across cast-on edge, then up right side seam edge to other marker, working 3 dc into each corner point, do **NOT** turn.
Now work 1 row of crab st (dc worked from left to right instead of right to left) along this edge. Fasten off.

Front and neck edging

Starting and ending at markers along front side seam edges, work edging along front cast-on edges, front openings edges and neck edge in same way as given for lower back edging.

Sleeve edgings (both alike)

Join sleeve seams.
Starting and ending at top of sleeve cuff opening, work edging along row-end edges of cuff opening and cast-on edge in same way as given for lower back edging.

Pocket edgings (both alike)

Work edging along pocket tops in same way as given for lower back edging.
Neatly sew pocket linings in place on inside. Join side seams. Sew sleeves into armholes. Using one strand of yarn, cover buttons following instructions on packet, then sew in place.

Recommendation
Suitable for the knitter with a little experience
Please see pages 51, 52 & 53 for photographs.

	XS	S	M	L	XL	XXL	
To fit	**81**	**86**	**91**	**97**	**102**	**109**	cm
bust	32	34	36	38	40	43	in

Rowan Pure Cashmere DK

| 8 | 9 | 10 | 10 | 11 | 11 | x 25gm |

Photographed in Cork

Needles
1 pair 3mm (no 11) (US 2/3) needles
1 pair 3¼mm (no 10) (US 3) needles

Buttons – 10

Tension
27 sts and 37 rows to 10 cm measured over
stocking stitch using 3¼mm (US 3) needles.

FAWN
UNDERSTATED CROPPED CLASSIC CARDIGAN

BACK
Cast on 95 (101: 107: 115: 121: 133) sts
using 3mm (US 2/3) needles.
Row 1 (RS): P1 (0: 1: 1: 0: 0), *K1, P1, rep
from * to last 0 (1: 0: 0: 1: 1) st, K0 (1: 0: 0:
1: 1).
Row 2: K1 (0: 1: 1: 0: 0), *P1, K1, rep from *
to last 0 (1: 0: 0: 1: 1) st, P0 (1: 0: 0: 1: 1).
These 2 rows form rib.
Cont in rib for a further 24 rows, inc 1 st at
each end of 15th of these rows and ending
with a WS row.
97 (103: 109: 117: 123: 135) sts.
Change to 3¼mm (US 3) needles.
Beg with a K row, now work in st st throughout
as folls:
Work 6 rows, ending with a WS row.
Next row (inc) (RS): K3, M1, K to last 3 sts,
M1, K3.
Working all side seam increases as set by last
row, inc 1 st at each end of 14th and 2 foll
14th rows.
105 (111: 117: 125: 131: 143) sts.
Cont straight until back measures 22 (22: 23:
23: 23: 23) cm, ending with a WS row.
Shape armholes
Cast off 3 (4: 4: 5: 5: 6) sts at beg of next
2 rows.
99 (103: 109: 115: 121: 131) sts.
Dec 1 st at each end of next 5 (5: 7: 7: 9: 11)
rows, then on foll 2 (3: 3: 4: 4: 6) alt rows,
then on foll 4th row.
83 (85: 87: 91: 93: 95) sts.
Cont straight until armhole measures 17 (18:
18: 19: 20: 21) cm, ending with a WS row.
Shape back neck and shoulders
Cast off 7 (7: 8: 8: 8: 9) sts at beg of next
2 rows.
69 (71: 71: 75: 77: 77) sts.
Next row (RS): Cast off 7 (7: 8: 8: 8: 9) sts,
K until there are 12 (12: 11: 12: 13: 12) sts
on right needle and turn, leaving rem sts on
a holder.
Work each side of neck separately.
Cast off 4 sts at beg of next row.
Cast off rem 8 (8: 7: 8: 9: 8) sts.
With RS facing, rejoin yarn to rem sts, cast off
centre 31 (33: 33: 35: 35: 35) sts, K to end.
Complete to match first side, reversing
shapings.

LEFT FRONT
Cast on 53 (56: 59: 63: 66: 72) sts using
3mm (US 2/3) needles.
Row 1 (RS): P1 (0: 1: 1: 0: 0), *K1, P1, rep
from * to last 6 sts, K6.
Row 2: Cast on 1 st, cast off 1 st (to form
picot), K until there are 7 sts on right needle,
*P1, K1, rep from * to last 0 (1: 0: 0: 1: 1) st,
P0 (1: 0: 0: 1: 1).
Row 3: As row 1.
Row 4: K7, *P1, K1, rep from * to last 0 (1: 0:
0: 1: 1) st, P0 (1: 0: 0: 1: 1).
These 4 rows set the sts - front opening edge
6 sts in g st with picots on every 4th row and
rem sts in rib.
Cont as set for a further 22 rows, inc 1 st at
beg of 13th of these rows and ending with
a WS row. 54 (57: 60: 64: 67: 73) sts.
Change to 3¼mm (US 3) needles.
Next row (RS): Knit.
Next row: Patt 6 sts, P to end.
These 2 rows set the sts for rest of left front -
front opening edge 6 sts still in g st with picot
trim but all other sts now in st st.
Keeping sts correct, cont as folls:
Work 4 rows, ending with a WS row.
Working all side seam increases as set by
back, inc 1 st at beg of next and 3 foll 14th
rows.
58 (61: 64: 68: 71: 77) sts.
Cont straight until left front matches back
to beg of armhole shaping, ending with
a WS row.
Shape armhole
Keeping sts correct, cast off 3 (4: 4: 5: 5: 6)
sts at beg of next row.
55 (57: 60: 63: 66: 71) sts.
Work 1 row.
Dec 1 st at armhole edge of next 5 (5: 7: 7: 9:
11) rows, then on foll 2 (3: 3: 4: 4: 6) alt rows,
then on foll 4th row.
47 (48: 49: 51: 52: 53) sts.
Cont straight until 20 (20: 20: 24: 24: 24)
rows less have been worked than on back
to beg of shoulder shaping, ending with
a WS row.
Shape front neck
Next row (RS): K33 (33: 34: 36: 37: 38) and
turn, leaving rem 14 (15: 15: 15: 15: 15) sts
on a holder.

Dec 1 st at neck edge of next 6 rows, then
on foll 4 alt rows, then on 1 (1: 1: 2: 2: 2)
foll 4th rows.
22 (22: 23: 24: 25: 26) sts.
Work 1 row, ending with a WS row.

Shape shoulder
Cast off 7 (7: 8: 8: 8: 9) sts at beg of next
and foll alt row.
Work 1 row.
Cast off rem 8 (8: 7: 8: 9: 8) sts.
Mark positions for 10 buttons along left front
opening edge - first button to come in row 5,
2nd button to come in row 23, top button to
come just above neck shaping, and rem
7 buttons evenly spaced between top button
and 2nd button.

RIGHT FRONT
Cast on 53 (56: 59: 63: 66: 72) sts using
3mm (US 2/3) needles.
Row 1 (RS): K6, *P1, K1, rep from * to last
1 (0: 1: 1: 0: 0) st, P1 (0: 1: 1: 0: 0).
Row 2: K1 (0: 1: 1: 0: 0), *P1, K1, rep from *
to last 6 sts, K6.
Row 3: Cast on 1 st, cast off 1 st (to form
picot), K until there are 6 sts on right needle,
*P1, K1, rep from * to last 1 (0: 1: 1: 0: 0) st,
P1 (0: 1: 1: 0: 0).
Row 4: As row 2.
These 4 rows set the sts - front opening edge
6 sts in g st with picots on every 4th row and
rem sts in rib.
Keeping sts correct as now set, cont as folls:
Row 5 (buttonhole row) (RS): Patt 2 sts,
K2tog tbl, yfwd, K to end.
Working a further 8 buttonholes in this way
to correspond with positions marked for
buttons on left front and noting that no
further reference will be made to buttonholes,
cont as folls:
Work 21 rows, inc 1 st at end of 12th of these
rows and ending with a WS row.
54 (57: 60: 64: 67: 73) sts.
Change to 3¼mm (US 3) needles.
Next row (RS): Patt 6 sts, K to end.
Next row: P to last 6 sts, K6.
These 2 rows set the sts for rest of
right front - front opening edge 6 sts
still in g st with picot trim but all other
sts now in st st.
Complete to match left front, reversing
shapings and working first row of neck
shaping as folls:
Shape front neck
Next row (RS): Patt 14 (15: 15: 15: 15: 15)
sts and slip these sts onto a holder, K to end.
33 (33: 34: 36: 37: 38) sts.

SLEEVES (both alike)
Cast on 49 (51: 53: 57: 59: 61) sts using
3mm (US 2/3) needles.
Row 1 (RS): P1, *K1, P1, rep from * to end.
Row 2: K1, *P1, K1, rep from * to end.
These 2 rows form rib.
Cont in rib for a further 28 rows, inc 1 st at
each end of 13th of these rows and foll 14th
row, and ending with a WS row.
53 (55: 57: 61: 63: 65) sts.
Change to 3¼mm (US 3) needles.
Beg with a K row and working all sleeve
increases in same way as side seam increases,
now work in st st, shaping sides by inc 1 st at
each end of 7th (7th: 9th: 11th: 9th: 9th) and
every foll 8th (8th: 10th: 12th: 10th: 10th) row
to 63 (61: 73: 83: 73: 71) sts, then on every
foll 10th (10th: 12th: -: 12th: 12th) row until
there are 79 (81: 81: -: 87: 89) sts.
Cont straight until sleeve measures 45 (46:
47: 48: 49: 50) cm, ending with a WS row.
Shape top
Cast off 3 (4: 4: 5: 5: 6) sts at beg of next
2 rows. 73 (73: 73: 73: 77: 77) sts.
Dec 1 st at each end of next 3 rows, then
on foll alt row, then on 6 (7: 7: 8: 7: 8) foll
4th rows. 53 (51: 51: 49: 55: 53) sts.
Work 1 row, ending with a WS row.
Dec 1 st at each end of next and foll 5 (4: 4: 3:
6: 5) alt rows, then on foll 3 rows, ending with
a WS row.
Cast off rem 35 sts.

MAKING UP
Press all pieces with a warm iron over a damp cloth.
Join both shoulder seams using back stitch or
mattress stitch if preferred.
Neckband
With RS facing and using 3mm (US 2/3)
needles, slip 14 (15: 15: 15: 15: 15) sts from
right front holder onto right needle, rejoin yarn
and pick up and knit 24 (24: 24: 28: 28: 28)
sts up right side of neck, 39 (41: 41: 43: 43:
43) sts from back, and 24 (24: 24: 28: 28: 28)
sts down left side of neck, then patt across 14
(15: 15: 15: 15: 15) sts on left front holder.
115 (119: 119: 129: 129: 129) sts.
Row 1 (WS): Patt 6 sts, K1, *P1, K1, rep from *
to last 6 sts, patt 6 sts.
This row sets the sts - front opening edge 6
sts (at both ends of rows) still in g st with picot
trim and rem sts in rib.
Making 10th buttonhole in next row, cont as
set for a further 5 rows, ending with a **RS** row.
Cast off in patt (on **WS**).
Join side seams. Join sleeve seams. Sew
sleeves into armholes. Sew on buttons.

38.5 (41: 43.5: 46: 48.5: 53) cm
15¼ (16: 17: 18: 19: 21) in

39 (40: 41: 42: 43: 44) cm
15 (15½: 16: 16½: 17: 17½) in

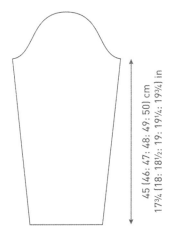

45 (46: 47: 48: 49: 50) cm
17¾ (18: 18½: 19: 19¼: 19¾) in

INFORMATION

TENSION

Achieving the correct tension has to be one of the most important elements in producing a beautiful, well fitting knitted garment. The tension controls the size and shape of your finished piece and any variation to either stitches or rows, however slight, will affect your work and change the fit completely.

To avoid any disappointment, we would always recommend that you knit a tension square in the yarn and stitch given in the pattern, working perhaps four or five more stitches and rows than those given in the tension note.

When counting the tension, place your knitting on a flat surface and mark out a 10cm square with pins. Count the stitches between the pins. If you have too many stitches to 10cm your knitting it too tight, try again using thicker needles, if you have too few stitches to 10cm your knitting is too loose, so try again using finer needles. Please note, if you are unable to achieve the correct stitches and rows required, the stitches are more crucial as many patterns are knitted to length.

Keep an eye on your tension during knitting, especially if you're going back to work which has been put to one side for any length of time.

SIZING

The instructions are given for the smallest size. Where they vary, work the figures in brackets for the larger sizes. One set of figures refers to all sizes. The size diagram with each pattern will help you decide which size to knit. The measurements given on the size diagram are the actual size your garment should be when completed.

Measurements will vary from design to design because the necessary ease allowances have been made in each pattern to give your garment the correct fit, i.e. a loose fitting

garment will be several cm wider than a neat fitted one, a snug fitting garment may have no ease at all.

WRAP STITCH

A wrap stitch is used to eliminate the hole created when using the short row shaping method. Work to the position on the row indicated in the pattern, wrap the next st (by slipping next st onto right needle, taking yarn to opposite side of work between needles and then slipping same st back onto left needle – on foll rows, K tog the loop and the wrapped st) and turn, cont from pattern.

BEADING

Bead 1 (RS rows) = place a bead by bringing yarn to front (RS) of work and slipping bead up next to st just worked, slip next st purlwise from left needle to right needle and return yarn to back (WS) of work, leaving bead sitting in front of slipped st on RS. Do not place beads on edge sts of rows as this will interfere with seaming and picking up sts.

Beading note

Before starting to knit, thread beads onto yarn. To do this, thread a fine sewing needle (one which will easily pass through the beads) with sewing thread. Knot ends of thread and then pass end of yarn through this loop. Thread a bead onto sewing thread and then gently slide it along and onto knitting yarn. Continue in this way until required numbers of beads are on yarn.

Working a lace pattern

When working a lace pattern it is important to remember that if you are unable to work a full repeat i.e. both the increase and corresponding decrease and vice versa, the stitches should be worked in stocking stitch or an alternative stitch suggested in the pattern.

FINISHING INSTRUCTIONS

It is the pressing and finishing which will transform your knitted pieces into a garment to be proud of.

Pressing

Darn in ends neatly along the selvage edge. Follow closely any special instructions given on the pattern or ball band and always take great care not to over press your work.

Block out your knitting on a pressing or ironing board, easing into shape, and unless otherwise states, press each piece using a warm iron over a damp cloth.

Tip: Attention should be given to ribs/edgings; if the garment is close fitting – steam the ribs gently so that the stitches fill out but stay elastic. Alternatively if the garment is to hang straight then steam out to the correct shape.

Tip: Take special care to press the selvages, as this will make sewing up both easier and neater.

CONSTRUCTION
Stitching together

When stitching the pieces together, remember to match areas of pattern very carefully where they meet. Use a stitch such as back stitch or mattress stitch for all main knitting seams and join all ribs and neckband with mattress stitch, unless otherwise stated.

Take extra care when stitching the edgings and collars around the back neck of a garment. They control the width of the back neck, and if too wide the garment will be ill fitting and drop off the shoulder.

Knit back neck edgings only to the length stated in the pattern, even stretching it slightly if for example, you are working in garter or horizontal rib stitch.

Stitch edgings/collars firmly into place using

a back stitch seam, easing-in the back neck to fit the collar/edging rather than stretching the collar/edging to fit the back neck.

CARE INSTRUCTIONS

Yarns

Follow the care instructions printed on each individual ball band. Where different yarns are used in the same garment, follow the care instructions for the more delicate one.

Buttons

We recommend that buttons are removed if your garment is to be machine washed.

CROCHET

We are aware that crochet terminology varies from country to country. Please note we have used the English style in this publication.

Crochet abbreviations

ch	chain
ss	slip stitch
dc	double crochet
tr	treble

Double crochet

1. Insert the hook into the work (as indicated in the pattern), wrap the yarn over the hook and draw the yarn through the work only.
2. Wrap the yarn again and draw the yarn through both loops on the hook.
3. 1 dc made

Treble

1. Wrap the yarn over the hook and insert the hook into the work (as indicated on the pattern).
2. Wrap the yarn over the hook draw through the work only and wrap the yarn again.
3. Draw through the first 2 loops only and wrap the yarn again.
4. Draw through the last 2 loops on the hook.
5. 1 treble made.

ABBREVIATIONS

K	knit
P	purl
K1b	knit 1 through back loop
st(s)	stitch(es)
inc	increas(e)(ing)
dec	decreas(e)(ing)
st st	stocking stitch (1 row K, 1 row P)
garter st	garter stitch (K every row)
beg	begin(ning)
foll	following
rem	remain(ing)
rev st st	reverse stocking stitch (1 row P, 1 row K)
rep	repeat
alt	alternate
cont	continue
patt	pattern
tog	together
mm	millimetres
cm	centimetres
in(s)	inch(es)
RS	right side
WS	wrong side
sl 1	slip one stitch
psso	pass slipped stitch over
tbl	through back of loop
M1	make one stitch by picking up horizontal loop before next stitch and knitting into back of it
M1p	make one stitch by picking up horizontal loop before next stitch and purling into back of it
yfwd	yarn forward (making a stitch)
yon	yarn over needle (making a stitch)
yrn	yarn round needle (making a stitch)-
MP	Make picot: Cast on 1 st, by inserting the right needle between the first and second stitch on left needle, take yarn round needle, bring loop through and place on left (one stitch cast on), cast off 1 st, by knitting first the loop and then the next stitch, pass the first stitch over the second (one stitch cast off).
Cn	cable needle
C4B	Cable 4 back: Slip next 2 sts onto a cn and hold at back of work, K2, K2 from cn.
C4F	Cable 4 front: Slip next 2 sts onto a cn and hold at front of work, K2, K2 from cn.

THANK YOU!

Firstly we would like to say a huge, huge thank you to Mark and Pauline for allowing us to shoot on their farm; it provided the most perfect setting for our photographs.

As always to our team of tremendous people without whose contributions this book would not be achieved. To Graham for his fantastic work on both the photography and editorial design, Angela for her skills on the page layouts, our gorgeous model Kristie, and Diana for her hair & make-up talents, Sue Whiting and Tricia for their pattern writing & checking expertise, our lovely knitters, Ella, Sandra, Joan, Margaret, Glennis and Ann, to Susan for finishing the garments so well, Helene and all at Revival www.revivalvintage.co.uk, and the whole team at Be Authentic www.b-authentic.co.uk. Also, to Kate, David, Ann, Margaret and the Rowan team for their constant support.

Finally thanks to Nigel and Lindsay for opening up their home, for putting up with our intrusion and for making us all feel so very welcome.

Kim & Kathleen

INDEX